Portugu

Learn Portuguese In 21 DAYS!

A Practical Guide To Make Portuguese Look Easy! EVEN For Beginners

Table of Contents

Introduction 4
Chapter 1: The Portuguese Alphabet 5
Chapter 2: Pronunciation Guide (1/2) 7
Chapter 3: Pronunciation Guide (2/2) 9
Chapter 4: Greetings and Basic Phrases 13
Chapter 5: Portuguese Numbers (Números) 16
Cardinal Numbers 17
Ordinal Numbers 20
Chapter 6: Months, Days, and Seasons 22
Chapter 7: Time and Date (Hora e Data) 24
Chapter 8: Colors in Portuguese (Cores) 29
Chapter 9: Word Order 30
Chapter 10: Capitalization and Punctuation 35
Chapter 11: Articles (Artigos) 37
Chapter 12: Nouns (Substantivos) 39
Masculine Nouns 39
Feminine Nouns 44
Chapter 13: Invariable Nouns 51
Forming Plural Nouns 53
Chapter 14: Pronouns (Pronomes) 65
Subject Pronouns (Pronomes Pessoais) 65
Direct Object Pronouns 67
Chapter 15: Reflexive Pronouns 70
Possessive Pronouns and Adjectives 71
Demonstrative Pronouns and Demonstrative Adjectives 72
Interrogative Pronouns 74
Chapter 16: Adjectives (Adjetivos) 76
Irregular Adjectives 78
Irregular Comparative and Superlative Forms 82
Most Commonly Used Portuguese Adjectives 83
Chapter 17: Verbs (Verbos) 85
The Indicative Mood Tenses 86
Imperative Mood 87

Subjunctive Mood 87
The Conditional Mood 94
Chapter 18: Adverbs (Advérbios) 110
Chapter 19: Prepositions (Preposições) 119
Chapter 20: Useful Phrases 127
Chapter 21: Vocabulary 141
Conclusion 152

Introduction

This book contains 21 highly-informative chapters on the fundamentals of Portuguese grammar and communication. Each chapter is designed to provide self-learners a complete yet compact learning material that will help them speak the language with ease in a very short time. It addresses the needs of travellers, students, entrepreneurs, and professionals for a grammar reference and phrase book in one resource.

Each chapter features tables, charts, and relevant examples to make learning the Portuguese language an interesting and enjoyable experience.

The first 8 chapters deal with the basic things every speaker should know: the alphabet, pronunciation, numbers, months and days, seasons, telling time and date, colors, and basic survival phrases for getting around in a Portuguese-speaking country.

The succeeding chapters deal with the essential aspects of grammar including sentence construction and the different parts of speech.

The book winds up with a chapter on key travel phrases and a final chapter of vocabulary listings for daily conversations.

Language learners will find this book an invaluable reference for learning the European and the Brazilian branches of the Portuguese language.

Let's begin the journey.

Chapter 1: The Portuguese Alphabet

Portuguese is a Roman language spoken in Portugal, Brazil, Mozambique, Angola, Guinea-Bissau, East Timor, São Tomé e Principe, Cape Verde, Macau, and Equatorial Guinea. It is also spoken by small communities in India and Malaysia.

Portuguese descended from the Latin language (Vulgar Latin) which became the predominant langauge at the time of the Roman invasion of the Iberian Peninsula. The language gradually evolved in the Atlantic coast territories into what was known as Galician-Portuguese language. It would later split in Galician and Portuguese languages when Galicia was incorporated into Spain and as Portugal developed independently. King Dinis I of Portugal decared the use of Portuguese language as the official language in 1290.

In 1911, Portugal adopted a reformed orthography, which introduced major changes in the spelling. The revised standard was used officially in Portugal and its then territories that included the now independent countries like Mozambique, Angola, East Timor, Cape Verde, São Tomé and Príncipe, Guinea-Bissau, Macau, Dadra and Nagar Haveli, and Goa, Diu, and Daman of India. Brazil would later adopt a slightly modified form of Portugal's orthography 1n 1943 which was eventually revised in 1970. In 2009, Brazil introduced a new orthography with the purpose of unifying written Portuguese among the lusophone countries. Its adoption in other Portuguese-speaking countries has not been set.

Portuguese is spoken by about 230 million people. Of this, about 190 million are from Brazil. There are notable differences between European Portuguese and Brazilian Portuguese in terms of pronunciation, spelling, and vocabulary but these are overshadowed by many similarities.

The Portuguese alphabet is Latin-based and consists of 23 letters. In addition, it uses three letters (k,w,y) excusively for foreign-derived words.

Letter	European Letter Name	Brazilian Letter Name
Aa	á	á
Bb	bê	bê
Cc	cê	cê
Dd	dê	dê
Ee	é	é or ê
Ff	efe	efe
Gg	gê or guê	gê
Hh	agá	agá
Ii	i	i
Jj	jota	jota
Kk	capa	cá
Ll	ele	ele
Mm	eme	eme
Nn	ene	ene
Oo	ó	ó or ô
Pp	pê	pê
Qq	quê	quê
Rr	erre or rê	erre
Ss	esse	esse
Tt	tê	tê
Uu	u	u
Vv	vê	vê
Ww	dâblio or duplo vê	dáblio or duplo vê
Xx	xis	xis
Yy	ípsilon or i grego	ípsilon
Zz	zê	zê

Chapter 2: Pronunciation Guide (1/2)

Diacritical marks are symbols that indicate how a word should be pronounced. In some cases, they are used to clarify a word's meaning and usage. The Portuguese language uses a number of diacritical marks.

Diacritical Marks

~	The tilde is used to indicate a nasal sound
´	An acute accent indicates stress on a syllable and an open vowel sound
^	A circumflex indicates stress and close vowel sound on the marked syllable
`	A grave (grahv) mark indicates contraction of two words
˛	A cedilla is used to denote soft (s sound) pronunciation for the letter "c"
¨	Diaresis or umlauts on the letter "u" denotes a "qw" and "gw" sound when placed after "q" and "g" respectively.

Acute (´) and circumflex (^) symbols are used to indicate stress on the marked syllables while the grave, cedilla, and diaeresis modify pronunciation. Tilde is only used to indicate nasal pronunciation and stress in words with ã ending. The diaeresis mark is now considered obsolete with the effectivity of the orthographic agreement in 2009. Its use is presently limited to borrowed words and personal names.

Vowel Sounds

Vowel Sounds		Sounds like:	Example
a	unstressed	the "a" in beta	santana
a	stressed before a nasal consonant	the "a" in beta	guarda
a	stressed before other consonants	the "a" in cat	crato
á	stressed a	the "a" in father	calix
ã	nasal sound	the "an" in angry	não
e	eh, unstressed	the "e" in net	loures
é	eh, stressed	the "e" in let	pinhel
ê	ey	the "ey" in they	bêbado
êm, em, ém	nasal sound	the "e" in end	em
i	ee	the "ee" in week	dizer
o	unstressed	the "oo" in loot but shorter	corvo
ó	stressed o	the "o" in law	próprio
ô	o	the "o" in sore	avô
õ		close to "on" in French bon	canções
u	oo	the "oo" in look	usar

Chapter 3: Pronunciation Guide (2/2)

Consonant Sounds

Consonants		Sounds like	Examples
b		the "b" in boy	borba
c	hard before a,o,u	the "c" in car	carro
c	soft before e,i	the "s" in sand	certo
ç	soft before a,o,u	the "s" in sun	aço
d		the "d" in desk	dar
d	between vowels	the "th" in this	idade
f		the "f" in fit	penafiel
g	hard before a,o,u	the "g" in go	gato
g	soft, before e,i	the "s" in leisure	gente
gu	hard before a,o,u	the "g" in get	água
gu	soft before e and i	the "g" in guide	guia
qu	hard before a,o,u	the "qu" in quick	quando
qu	soft before e and i	the "qu" in quiche	que
h		silent at the start of a word	
j		the "su" in pleasure	já
l		the "l" in leap	alandroal
m		the "m" in money	mafra
n		the "n" in	alcanena

		nine	
p		the "p" in port	porto
q		the "k" in kit	ourique
r	start of a word/before a nasal vowel	a rolled "r" similar to Spanish	rico
r	syllable coda/after consonant or non-nasal vowel	"dd" in ladder	Rio Maior
rr		trilled sound	ferro
s	start of a word, before s	the "s" in sun at the start of a word	si
s	before a voiceless consonant	the "sh" in she	estar
s	at the end of a word	the "sh" in she	dois
s	between vowels	the "z" in zoo	asa
t		the "t" in ten	tomar
v		the "v" in vine	viseu
x	word initial, after j	the "sh" in she	seixal
x	start of a word	before a vowel, the "s" in same	máximo
x	start of a syllable	the "z" in zoo	Nazaré
x	middle of a word	between vowels, the "x" in taxi	taxi
z		the "z" in zest	luzes

z	end of a word	the "sh" in she	luz

Letter Combinations

Digraph	Context	English sounds	Example
ch		like "sh" in show	machico
sc	before e or i	like "sh" in she	descer
lh		like "lli" in million.	batalha
nh		like "ny" in canyon	cantanhede
gu	before e or i	like "g" in go.	felgueiras
	before a or o/ before e or i	like "Gw" in Gwen.	mortágua
qu	before e or i	like "k" in skip	monchique
	before a or o/ before e or i	like "qu" in quite.	quatro
rr	trilled sound	no equivalent	parra
ss		like "s" in since.	osso

Dipthongs

Dipthongs	Sounds like
au	"ow" in cow
ia	"ia" in Lydia
io	"ew" in new
ei	"ay" in play
oa	"oa" in boa
oe	"we" in wet
oi	"wee" in weed

ou	"oo" in look
ua	"wa" in water
ui	"we" in week

Chapter 4: Greetings and Basic Phrases

Bom dia!	bon DEE-ah	Good day!
Olá!	O-lá	Hello! (informal)
Como está?	KOH-moh ish-TAH?	How are you?
Então? tudo bem? (coll.-Port.)	eng-ta-ong? too-doo bah-ing?	So, what's up?
Oi! e aí? (colloquial-Brazil)	oy? ee ah-ee	So, what's up?
Tudo Bem.	TOO-do BENG	Everything is fine.
Bem/muito bem	Baing/moo-ee-toh baing	Well/Very well.
Bem, obrigado/a	BENG, ob-ree-GAH-doo/dah	Fine, thank you
Mal/muito mal	Mao/moo-ee-toh mao	Bad/Very bad.
Mais ou menos	Ma-eece oh meh-nos	More or less, so-so
Obrigado. (if you're a man)	ob-ree-GAH-doo	Thank you.
Obrigada. (if you're a woman)	ob-ree-GAH-dah	Thank you.
De nada	je NAH-dah	You're welcome.
Como está?	KOH-moh ish-TAH?	How are you?
Como vai?	Coh-moh vye?"	How's it going?
Como se chama?	KOH-moh se SHA-ma?	What is your name?
(O) meu nome é _____	(oh) mew NOME ey _____	My name is _____
Muito prazer em conhecê-lo	MOOY-to pra-ZEHR eng koh-nye-SEH-lo	Nice to meet you.

Portuguese	Pronunciation	English
Sim.	SEE (Portugal)/SEEN (Brazil)	Yes.
Não.	NOWNG	No.
Desculpe.	desh-KULP (Port)/desh-KUL-pay(Brazil)	I'm sorry.
Com licença!	co-lee-sensah	Excuse me.
Não faz mal!	nah-fash-mahl	No problem./No worries.
Está bem!	tah baing	It's okay./That's enough.
Por favor	pohr fa-VOHR	Please
Até logo.	ah-TEH LOH-goo	See you later.
Até mais!	ah-tay myee-sh	See you soon.
Adeus!	uh-DEOOSH	Goodbye!
Tchau!	CHOW	Goodbye! (informal)
Não falo Português.	NOWNG fah-loo por-too-GEZH	I can't speak Portuguese.
Fala Inglês?	fah-lah ing-GLEZH?	Do you speak English?
Socorro!	soo-KOO-hoo!	Help!
Bom dia!	bon DEE-ah	Good day!
Boa tarde!	bo-ah/TARD(Port)/TAR-day(Brazil)	Good evening!
Boa noite!	bo-ah NOIT(Port)/NOI-chay(Brazil)	Good night!
Não sei!	naw say	I don't know
Não compreendo.	NOWNG kom-pre-EN-doo	I don't understand it.
Não percebi!	naw pehr-say-bee	I didn't understand it.

Não entendo! (Brazil)	naw en-tehn-doo	I don't understand it.
Não entendi! (Brazil)	naw en-tehn-chee	I didn't understand it.
Pode repetir?	pod ray-peh-teer?	Could you repeat, please?

Chapter 5: Portuguese Numbers (Números)

Numbering Rules

Numbers from zero to fifteen are specific words that must be memorized: (0)zero. (1) um, (2) dois, (3) três, (4) quatro, (5) cinco, (6) seis, (7) sete, (8) oito, (9) nove, (10) dez, (11) onze, (12) doze, (13) treze, (14) catorze, (15) quinze.

Numbers from sixteen to nineteen are obtained by combining ten and the unit: (10 and 6) dezasseis, (10 and 7) dezassete, (10 and 8) dezoito, and (10 and 9) dezanove.

Except for 10 and 20, the names of the tens are derived from the unit's root: (10) dez, (20) vinte, (30) trinta, (40) quarenta., (50) cinquenta, (60) sessenta, (70) setenta, (80) oitenta and (90) noventa.

The same rule applies when naming the hundreds: (100) cem/centos (plural), (200) duzentos, (300) trezentos, (400) quatrocentos, (500) quinhentos, (600) seiscentos, (700) setecentos, (800) oitocentos, and (900) novecentos.

An "e" (and) is used to connect tens and units (trinta e dois, 32) and hundred and tens (duzentos trinta e dois, 232). It is not, however, used to link thousands and hundreds except when the number ends with 2 zeroes (quarto mil e duzentos – 4,200). Thousands and units are also linked by "e" (dois mil e quarto – 2004).

In Portuguese you separate the thousands from the hundred and the millions from the thousands with a period or "pontos" while you set the decimal numbers apart with a comma or "vírgulas". Hence:

English -> Portuguese: 23,253,215.54 -> 23.253.215,54

Cardinal Numbers

0	zero	(zeh-ro)
1	um (m) uma (f)	um (oon) / uma (oo-mah)
2	dois (m) duas (f)	(doh-eesh) / duas (doo-ash)
3	três	(treh-sh) or (tray-eess - Brazil)
4	quarto	(kwa-troo)
5	cinco	(cin-koo)
6	seis	(say-eesh)
7	sete	(set) or (se-chee -Brazil)
8	oito	(oy-too)
9	nove	(noh-vee)
10	dez (uma dezena)	(desh) or (day-iss - Brazil)
11	onze	(on-zee)
12	doze (uma dúzia)	(doh-zee)
13	treze	(tray-zee)
14	quatorze, catorze	(ka-tor-zee)
15	quinze	(keen-zee)
16	dezesseis	(deh-zah-say-eesh) / (deh-zeh-seiss-Brazil.)
17	dezessete	(deh-zah-set) / (chee-zeh-seh-chee-Brazil)
18	dezoito	(deh-zoy-too) / (chee-zoy-too - Brazil)
19	dezenove	(deh-zah-nov) / (chee-zeh-noh-vee -

17

		Brazil)
20	vinte	(veent) or (veen-tchee) in Brazil
21	vinte e um (m) vinte e uma (f)	(veent e oon/oo-mah)
30	trinta	(treen-tah)
31	trinta e um (m) trinte e uma (f)	(treen-tah e oon/oo-mah)
32	trinta e dois (m) trinta e duas	(treen-tah e doh-eesh/doo-ash)
40	quarenta	(kwa-ren-tah)
50	cinqüenta	(cin-kwen-tah)
60	sessenta	(seh-sen-tah)
70	setenta	(seh-tayn-tah)
80	oitenta	(oy-tayn-tah)
90	noventa	(noo-vayn-tah)
100	cem (uma centena)	(saing] or [seh-ing] in Brazil)
101	cento e um (m) cento e uma (f)	(cen-too e oon or cen-too e oo-mah)
200	duzentos (m) duzentas (f)	(doo-zayn-toosh)
300	trezentos (m) trezentas (f)	(treh-zayn-toosh)
400	quatrocentos (m) quatrocentas (f)	(kwa-tro-cen-toos)
500	quinhentos (m) quinhentas (f)	(keen-nyientoosh)
600	seiscentos (m) seiscentas (f)	(seh-eesh-cen-toosh]
700	setecentos (m) setecentas (f)	(seh-tay-cen-toosh
800	oitocentos (m) oitocentas (f)	(oy-toh-cen-toosh
900	novecentos (m) novecentas (f)	(noh-vay-cen-toosh)

1000	mil (um milhar)	(meal) or (mee-oo) in Braz
1100	mil e cem	(meal e saing) or (mee-oo she-ing - Brazil)
1200	mil e duzentos	(meal e doo-zayn-toosh)
1235	mil duzentos e trinta e cinco	(meal doo-zayn-toosh e treen-tah e cin-koo)
2000	dois mil (m) duas mil (f)	(doh-eesh mil / (doo-ash meal)
1300	mil e trezentos	(meal e treh-zayn-toosh)
1 million	um milhão	(ung mee-lyee-aung)
2 million	dois milhões	(doh-eesh mee-lyee-oingsh)
3 million	três milhões	(traysh mee-lyee-oingsh)
1 billion	um bilhão / um bilhão (Brazil)	(ung bee-lyee-aung)
1 billion	dois biliões	(doh-eesh bee-lyee-oingsh)

Ordinal Numbers

Ordinal numbers follow the rules governing adjectives. When referring to feminine pronoun, for instance, ordinal numbers take an –a ending.

Examples:

a primeira filha -> the first daughter

o primeiro namorado -> the first boyfriend

When necessary, ordinal numbers may take plural endings.

Examples:

os primeiros anos -> the first years

os primeiros passos -> the first steps

When indicating a century, Portuguese speakers would not normally use the ordinal numbers. Instead, it is more common to hear "o século vinte e um" (the century 21) than "o vigésimo primeiro século " (the 21st century). In Portuguese, centuries are written in Roman numerals. Hence, the 21st century is expressed as "o século XXI".

The ordinal numbers usually precede the noun they modify.

Ordinal Numbers:

1st	primeiro	pre-may-roh
2nd	segundo	seh-goon-doh
3rd	terceiro	ter-say-roh
4th	quarto	ku-ar-toh
5th	quinto	keen-toh

6th	sexto	says-toh
7th	sétimo	seh-chee-moh
8th	oitavo	oy-tah-voh
9th	nono	noh-nu
10th	décimo	dess-ee-moh
11th	décimo primeiro	dess-ee-moh-pre-may-roh
12th	décimo Segundo	dess-ee-moh-seh-goon-doh
13th	décimo terceiro	dess-ee-moh-ter-say-roh
14th	décimo quarto	dess-ee-moh-ku-ar-toh
15th	décimo quinto	dess-ee-moh-keen-toh
16th	décimo sexton	dess-ee-moh-says-toh
17th	décimo sétimo	dess-ee-moh-she-chee-moh
18th	décimo oitavo	dess-ee-moh-oy-tah-voh
19th	décimo nono	dess-ee-moh-noh-nu
20th	vigésimo	vee-gess-ee-moh
30th	trigésimo	tree-gess-ee-moh
40th	quadragésimo	kuah-dra-gess-ee-moh
50th	qüinquagésimo	ku-een-ku-ah-gess-ee-moh
60th	sexagésimo	says-tah-gess-ee-moh
70th	septuagésimo	sep-too-ah-gess-ee-moh
80th	octogésimo	ock-tah-gess-ee-moh
90th	nonagésimo	noh-nah-gess-ee-moh
100th	centésimo	sen-tess-ee-moh

Chapter 6: Months, Days, and Seasons

Months of the Year (Os meses do ano)

janeiro	January
fevereiro	February
março	March
abril	April
maio	May
junho	June
julho	July
agosto	August
setembro	September
outubro	October
novembro	November
dezembro	December

Days of the Week (Os dias da semana)

domingo	Sunday
segunda-feira	Monday
terça-feira	Tuesday
quarta-feira	Wednesday
quinta-feira	Thursday
sexta-feira	Friday
sábado	Saturday

The seasons of the Year (As estações do ano)

primavera	spring
verão	summer
outono	autumn/fall
inverno	winter

Chapter 7: Time and Date (Hora e Data)

Asking the time

To ask for time, you can use any of the following questions and they all mean "What time is it?"

Que horas são?

Por favor, que horas são?

Que hora é ele?

To ask for time in a more formal manner:

Você sabe que horas são?

Telling Time

Telling time in Portuguese is quite simple and a lot like telling time in English. Just say the "hour number, the word "e" (and), and the minute number. Hence, to say 7:20:

São sete (horas) e vinte (minutos). -> It's seven twenty.

Take note that the horas and minutes are optional.

To express an exact hour:

São seis horas./São seis horas em ponto.

It's six o'clock./It's 6:00 sharp.

Time is always expressed in the plural except when it is at one o'clock when you have to say "É uma hora." For the rest, you'll use "São". Both are forms of the verb "ser" (to be).

To express "half an hour", you will use the expression "e meia". Hence:

São sis e meia. -> It's 6:30.

To tell time after the half hour, it is more common to say the remaining minutes before the approaching hour and to use the expression "para as" before the coming hour.

Example:

São vinte para as seis. -> It's twenty to six.

São cinco para as sete. -> It's five to seven.

To express time which is not specific, you can use the following expressions:

É meio-dia. -> It's noon.

É meia-noite. -> It's midnight.

Instead of using "am" or "pm" to describe the specific time, it is more common to use the expressions "da manhã" (in the morning), "da tarde" (in the afternoon), or da noite"(of the evening). To state an event that will occur at an exact time, the preposition "às" which means "at" is used before the hour.

Example:

O jogo começa às 7:00 da manhã. -> The game stars at 7:00 in the morning.

To state that an event will begin and end at a certain time, you use the expression "das (horas) (horas)" or "das (horas) até as (horas)".

O jogo será das 7:00 até às 9:00.

The game will be from seven to nine

O jogo será das 7:00 até às 9:00.

The game will be from seven till seven.

Time -> Expression -> English

11:50 a.m. -> São dez para as doze. -> It's ten to twelve.

2:15 a.m. -> São dois e quinze. -> It's quarter pass two.

7:10 a.m. -> sete seis. -> It's ten past seven.

1:25 p.m. -> Um venti e cinco da tarde. -> It's one twenty five pm.

at 8 (sharp) -> Em oito. -> It's 8 o'clock.

9:30 p.m. -> São nove e meia. -> It's nine and a half.

It is also common for people to use the 24-hour format, which is just a matter of subtracting 12 hours from the given time to get the usual 12-hour format.

For example:

São quinze e vinte e dois. -> It's three twenty-two PM.

São dezenove e quinze. -> It's seven fifteen PM.

uma reunião	a meeting
um compromisso	an appointment
uma consulta	a consultation
um encontro	a date
o relógio	the clock/the watch

O ônibus passa às sete e venti e cinco. There is a bus at seven twenty-five.

Minha aula começa às oito e meia. My classes begin at 8:30.

Writing Dates

To write dates in Portuguese, you have to write in this order: the day first, the month, and then the year. To write the date in the long format, you will use the preposition "de" (of) between the day and the month. Remember to always write the year in full. Dates are never separated by a comma.

Examples:

24 abril 2015

25 de dezembro 2015

Time Expressions:

agora	now
depois	later
antes	before
manhã	morning
tarde	afternoon
fim de tarde	evening
hoje	today
ontem	yesterday
amanhã	tomorrow
esta semana	this week
semana passada	last week
próxima semana	next week

Chapter 8: Colors in Portuguese (Cores)

Like other adjectives, most colors in Portuguese must change their ending to agree with the number and gender of the noun they describe. Adjectives ending in –o must change to an –a ending when describing a feminine noun. Adjectives ending in –a need not change to –o when describing a masculine noun. When forming plural, most adjectives add an –s to the singular form.

Examples:

a casa branca	the white house
as casas amarelas	the yellow houses
o envelope verde	the green envelope
os carros azuis	the blue cars.

Most common colors:

vermelho (ver-MEH-lyoo)	red
azul (ah-ZOOL), pl. azuis (ah-ZOOEYSH)	blue
amarelo (ah-mah-REH-loo)	yellow
laranja (lah-RANG-jah)	orange
verde (VEHR-deh (Port.)	green
verde VEHR-day (Brazil)	green
verde VEHR-jay (Rio))	green
castanho (cah-STAHN-yo)	brown
preto (PREH-too)	black
branco (BRAHNG-koo)	white
cinzento (see-ZHEN-toh)	gray
violeta (vee-oh-LAY-tah)	purple

Chapter 9: Word Order

The basic word order in Portuguese is similar to English: Subject-Verb-Object. Portuguese, however, is more flexible than English and it's not unusual to see non-subject words at the beginning of a sentence.

The subject-verb-object word order can be used when forming statements, direct questions, indirect questions, and negative statements.

Statements

A statement is used when expressing an event or a fact. It uses the Subject-Verb-Object pattern. Take a look at a basic statement in Portuguese:

	Subject	Verb	Object	Prepositional Phrase
Portuguese	Nós	comemos	bolo	na festa.
English	We	ate	cake	at the party.

Portuguese	Ele	tem	um trabalho	na França.
English	He	has	a job	in France.

Just by using this simple word order, you can easily form your own sentences in Portuguese.

Direct Questions

Forming a simple direct question is just as easy. All you have to do is use a question word and follow it with a statement using the subject-verb-object order.

First, here are common question words in Portuguese:

Quem	Who
Qual	What
O que	What
Onde	Where
Quando	When
Por que	Why
De quem	Whose
Com quem	With whom
Sobre quem	About whom
Quantos	How many
À que horas	At what time
Por que não	Why not
Qual	Which one
Aonde	To where
A quem	To whom
Para onde	To where
De onde	From where
Quanto	How much
Por que você não	Why don't you

	Question Word	Subject	Verb	Object
Portuguese	Onde	ele	compra	livros?
English	Where	does he	buy	books?
Portuguese	O que	ela	faz	na Franca?
English	What	does	do	in

		she		France?

When speaking, you must raise your intonation at the end of the question.

Indirect Questions

In Portuguese, indirect questions follow the same word order as statements but they end with a question mark amk end with a rising intonation. Portuguese indirect questions do not start with a verb unlike those in English.

Here are some examples of indirect questions:

	Subject	Verb	Object	Prep. Phrase
Portuguese	Ele	tem	um trabaho	na Franca?
English	Does he	have	a job	in France?

	Subject	Verb	Object	Prep. Phrase
Portuguese	Nós	comemos	bolo	na festa?
English	Did we	eat	cake	at the party?

Negative sentences

A negative sentence expresses denial or disagreement. To form negative sentences, the word order remains the same but this time, a negative word is placed before the verb.

Negative words:

não	no, don't
ninguém	nobody, (not) anybody
nada	nothing, (not) anything
nenhum(a)	no, none
nem	nor
tampouco	neither, either
nem...nem	neither... nor
nunca, jamais	never, ever
nem sequer	not even

Here are some examples:

Subject	Negative	Verb	Object/Prep. Phrase
Nós	não	estamos comendo	bolo.
We	are not	eating	cake.
Eu	não	estou lendo	um livro.
I	am no	reading	a book.

Descriptive sentences

There is a big difference between English and Portuguese in word order when it comes to sentences with descriptive words. In English, adjectives are placed before the noun. In Portuguese, they are placed after the noun.

Here are some examples of sentences with two adjectives. Take note of the placement of the first adjective.

	Subject+Adjective	Verb	Adjective
Portuguese	O carro azul	é	caro.
English	The blue car	is	expensive.

	Subject+Adjective	Verb	Adjective
Portuguese	O rapaz alto	é	inteligente.
English	The tall boy	is	intelligent.

Chapter 10: Capitalization and Punctuation

Portuguese and English differ in several aspects of capitalization and punctuation. Here are basic Portuguese rules on capitalization and punctuation:

The following are capitalized:

Personal names

holidays

abbreviations

names of places

The days of the week are not capitalized on Portuguese.

Seasons of the year are capitalized in Portuguese.

In general, words that indicate nationalities are not capitalized.

Months of the year and academic subjects are capitalized in European Portuguese but not in Brazilian Portuguese.

Dates are not separated by a comma. For example: 30 de Maio de 2015.

Punctuation Marks (Pontuação)

Sign	Name
(.)	ponto (period)
(,)	Vírgula (comma)
(;)	Ponto e vírgula (semi-colon)
(:)	dois pontos (colon)
(?)	Ponto de interrogação (Question mark)
(!)	Ponto de exclamação (Exclamation mark)
(...)	Reticências (Suspension points)
("...")	Aspas (Inverted commas)
(...)	Parênteses (Brackets)
(-)	Travessão (Dash)

Chapter 11: Articles (Artigos)

Articles define the specificity or non-specificity of a noun. Unlike their equivalent in English, Portuguese articles agree with the number and gender of the noun they modify.

There are two main categories of articles: the definite articles and the indefinite articles. The definite articles are the equivalent of "the" in English while the indefinite articles are the equivalent of "a", "an", "any", "the" or "some". There are four definite articles and indefinite articles which correspond to the masculine and feminine gender as well as to the singularity or plurality of a noun.

Articles almost always precede a noun and it is not usual for Portuguese sentences to start with a noun. Definite articles, in particular, are more frequently used in Portuguese than in English. It's common to see definite articles before nouns referring to subjects like "a história"(History) or "a biologia" (Biology) in Portuguese. Definite articles are likewise prevalently used before proper nouns for people or places. Thus, it is common to see "os Estados Unidos" (the United States) or "o Francisco" (the Francisco). The use of definite articles before a proper noun is mostly defined by tradition. For instance, they are never used with proper nouns like Portugal, Timor, Moçambique, Angola or Cabo Verde.

Here are the articles and examples of their usage:

The definite articles (artigos definidos)

5Gender	Meaning	Singular	Plural
Masculine	the	o	os
Feminine	the	a	as

Examples:

o banho	the bath
a comida	the food
os gatos	the cats
as flores	the flowers

The indefinite articles (artigos indefinidos)

Gender	Meaning	Singular	Plural
Masculine	a, an, some	um	uns
Feminine	a, an, some	uma	umas

Examples:

um livro	a book
uns carros	some cars
uma bebida	a drink
umas cortinas	some curtains

Chapter 12: Nouns (Substantivos)

Nouns are words that name persons, things, places, ideas, or events. Nouns may be masculine or feminine and singular or plural. Modifiers like adjectives and articles must agree with the gender and number of the noun they modify.

Gender of Nouns

There are only two genders in Portuguese: the masculine and feminine genders. In many cases, it is possible to determine a noun's gender by its ending. Here are guidelines for identifying whether a noun is masculine or feminine:

Masculine Nouns

1. *Nouns ending in an unstressed –o are generally masculine.*

o ano	the year
o tio	the uncle
o carro	the car
o primo	the cousin
o amigo	the male friend
o marido	the husband

Exception: a foto (the photo), a tribo (the tribel)

2. *There are groups of masculine nouns that end with –a :*

In general, nouns ending in a stressed –a are masculine

o gala	the leading man
o imã	the magnet
o chá	the tea
o talisman	the talisman
o pá	shovel, mate
o cardigan	the cardigan
o sofá	the sofa

Exception: a lã (the wool), a maçã (the apple)

Masculine nouns ending in an unstressed –a:

o guia	the guide
o mapa	the map
o planeta	the planet
o dia	the day

Portuguese nouns ending in –ma which are of Greek origin are masculine nouns:

o sistema	the system
o programma	the program
o telefonema	the telephone call
o drama	the drama
o diagram	the diagram
o miasma	the decay
o clima	the climate

3. In general, nouns which end in –me are masculine.

o nome	the name
o legume	the vegetable
o costume	the custom
o volume	the volume
o uniforme	the uniform
o cume	the top, summit
o exame	the exam
o lume	the fire, the light
o queixume	the lament

Exceptions: a vexame (the shame or disgrace), a fome (the hunger)

4. In general, nouns ending in –r are masculine.

o prazer	the pleasure
o colar	the necklace
o motor	the motor
o lar	the home
o andar	the floor, storey
o humor	the humor
o ar	the air
o par	the pair, couple
o ardor	the ardour, passion
o furor	the fury, rage
o aspirador	the vacuum cleaner
o mar	the sea
o bar	the bar

Exceptions: a colher (the spoon), a mulher (the woman), a dor (the pain)

Nouns ending in –l are masculine.

o caracol	the snail
o hotel	the hotel
o hospital	the hospital
o canil	the kennel
o mel	the honey
o casal	the couple
o perfil	the profile
o fossil	the fossil
o reptile	the reptile
o anel	the ring
o lençol	the sheet
o futebol	the football
o painel	the panel, picture
o fuzil	the rifle
o papel	the paper
o textile	the textile

Nouns which end in –m are masculine.

o trem	the train
o patim	the skate
o jardim	the garden
o capim	the grass
o talharim	the tagliatelle or noodles

Some masculine nouns may apply to feminine nouns.

o cônjuge	the spouse
o animal	the animal
o indivíduo	the individual
o anjo	the angel

Feminine Nouns

Nouns ending in –ade and –ide are feminine.

a cidade	the city
a juventude	the youth
a amizade	the friendship
a virtude	the virtue
a igualdade	the equality
a tranquilidade	the tranquillity
a piedade	the pity
a nacionalidade	the nationality
a prioridade	the priority
a universidade	the university

Nouns which end in –gem are feminine

a margem	the margin
a engrenagem	the car's gear
a paragem	the stop
a homenagem	the tribute, homage
a ferragem	the hardwear
a viagem	the journey
a folhagem	the foliage
a malandragem	the cunning, double-dealing

Nouns which end in -são, –ção, –gião or – stão which correspond the English suffixes –sion, -tion, -gion, or –stion are feminine

a intenção	the intention
a mansão	the mansion
a erudição	the learning
a evasão	the evasion
a lição	the lesson
a nação	the nation
a ilustração	the illustration
a razão	the reason
a congestão	the congestion
a posição	the position
a religião	the religion
a imitação	the imitation
a confusão	the confusion
a ilusão	the illusion
a decisão	the decision
a região	the region
a combustão	the combustion
a sessão	the session

Exception: o coração (the heart)

Nouns which end in –cie are feminine.

a planície	the plain
a imundície	the filth
a superfície	the surface
a velhice	the old age
a meninice	the childhood

Some feminine nouns may apply to masculine gender.

a besta	the beast, animal
a vítima	the victim
a criança	the child

a testemunha	the witness
a pessoa	the person

Nouns ending in –e, z, and ão are either masculine or feminine

Since it's not possible to determine the gender by the noun's ending, it will be necessary to familiarize yourself with the gender of nouns with –e, -z, and –ão ending. Here are some nouns with these endings:

Nouns ending in –e

Masculine Nouns ending in –e

o envelope	the envelope
o peixe	the fish
o chicote	the whip
o cárcere	the prison
o leste	the east
o cheque	the cheque
o recorte	the cutting, clip
o desfile	the procession
o pé	the foot
o esmalte	the nail polish
o sangue	the blood
o ente	the being
o satellite	the satellite
o gabinete	the office
o traje	the dress, suit
o limite	the limit
o resgate	the ransom
o monte	the hill, pile
o parente	the relative

Feminine Nouns Ending in –e

a greve	the strike
a frase	the sentence
a mercê	the mercy
a tarde	the afternoon
a lente	the lens
a frente	the front
a massacre	the massacre
a gafe	the gaffe
a mare	the tide

Nouns which end in –z

Masculine nouns ending in -z

o xadrez	the chess
o xerez	the sherry
o cartaz	the bill, poster
o arroz	the rice

Feminine nouns ending in –z

a palidez	the paleness
a luz	the light
a matriz	the mould, womb
a maciez	the softness

Nouns ending in –ão

Masculine Nouns ending in –ão

o trovão	the thunder
o avião	the aeroplane
o travão	the brake
o escorregão	the slip-up
o volcão	the volcano
o pão	the bread

Feminine nouns ending in –ão

a vastidão	the immensity
a escuridão	the darkness
a mão	the hand
a escravidão	the slavery

Irregular Masculine and Feminine Nouns

Nationalities, Professions, relatives, animals, titles

poet	o poeta	poet	a poetisa
judge	o juiz	judge	a juiza
champion	o campeão	champion	a campeã
citizen	o cidadão	citizen	a cidadã
Jew	o judeu	Jew	a judeia
German	o alemão	German	a alemã
European	o europeu	European	a europeia
Catalan	o catalão	Catalan	a catalã
hero	o herói	heroine	a heroina
father	o pai	mother	a mãe
grandfather	o avô	grandmother	a avó
husband	o marido	wife	a esposa
father-in-law	o sogro	mother-in-law	a sogra
son-in-law	o genro	daughter-in-law	a genra
brother	o irmão	sister	a irmã
stepfather	o padrasto	stepmother	a madrasta
boy	o rapaz	girl	a rapariga (Pt)
actor	o ator	actress	a atriz
ambassador	o embaixador	ambassador	a embaixatriz
monk	o monge	nun	a monja

king	o rei	queen	a rainha
prince	o príncipe	princess	a princesa
duke	o duque	duchess	a duquesa
count	o conde	countess	a condesa
baron	o barão	baroness	a baronesa
gentleman	o cavaleiro	lady	a dama
bull/cow	o boi	bull/cow	a vaca
cock	o galo	hen	a galinha
dog	o cão	bitch	a cadela/ cachorra

Chapter 13: Invariable Nouns

Some nouns don't change in form whether they refer to male or female. Their gender is determined by the definite or indefinite article placed before them.

o/a criança	the child
o/a camarada	the comrade
o/a cobra	the snake
o/a colega	the colleague, classmate
o/a guia	the guide
o/a carioca	the Rio de Janeiro native
o/a indígena	the indigenous people
o/a cliente	the customer, client
o/a patriota	the patriot
o/a jovem	the young person
o/a homicídio	the homicide
o/a burocrata	the bureaucrat
o/a suicídio	the suicide, murdered person
o/a taxista	the taxi driver
o/a democrata	the democrat
o/a gerente	the manager, boss
o/a canadense	the Canadian
o/a cadete	the cadet
o/a estadunense	the American
o/a estudante	the student
o/a timorense	the Timorese
o/a intérprete	the interpreter
o/a artista	the artist

o/a tenista	the tennis player
o/a motorista	the driver
o/a doente	the ill person, invalid

Forming Plural Nouns

In general, Portuguese nouns form their plural by changing the ending of the noun's singular form. Following are the rules which govern the change in the noun's ending to form the plural:

Nouns ending in a vowel

Nouns ending in a vowel form their plural by adding –s to the singular form.

a amiga (friend) -> as amigas (the friends)

o ovo (the egg) -> os ovo (the eggs)

o peru (the turkey) -> os perus (the turkeys)

a árvore (the tree) -> as árvores (the trees)

Nouns ending in diphthongs likewise form their plural by adding s. The exceptions are nouns ending in –ão,

o judeu (the Jew) -> os judeus (the Jews)

o boi (the ox) -> os bois (the oxen)

o herói (the hero) -> os heróis (the heroes)

o céu (the sky) -> os cues (the skies)

a lei (the law)-> as leis (the laws)

Nouns ending in –m

Nouns which end in –m form their plural by changing –m to –n and adding s

o homem (the man) -> homens (the men)

a paisagem (the landscape) -> as paisagens (the landscapes)

a margem (the margin) -> as margens (the margins)

o jardim (the garden) -> os jardins (the gardens)

Nouns ending in –n

Nouns which end in –n form their plural by adding –s

o germen (the germ) -> os germens (the germs)

Nouns ending in –r or –z

Nouns with –r or –z ending form their plural by adding –es

a mulher (the woman) -> as mulheres (the women)

o rapaz (the boy) -> os rapazes (the boys)

o motor (the motor) -> os motores (the motors)

a colher (the spoon) -> as colheres (the spoons)

o cartaz (the poster) -> os cartazes (the posters)

a atriz (the actress) -> as atrizes (the actresses)

Nouns ending in –s

When the stress falls on the last syllable, nouns which end in –s form their plural by adding –es.

o país (the country) -> os países (the countries)

o dues (the god) -> os deuses (the gods)

o mês(the month) -> os meses (the months)

Take note that the noun drops the circumflex when it forms the plural. This rule works with nouns of many nationalities:

o ingles (the English) -> os ingleses (the English)

o francês (the French) -> os franceses (the French)

o português (the Portuguese) -> os portugueses (the Portuguese)

o chinês (the Chinese) -> os chineses (the Chinese)

If the stress falls on a syllable other than the final syllable, nouns ending in –s retain the singular form and are only modified by the accompanying article.

o lapis (the pencil) -> os lapis (the pencils)

o atlas (the atlas) -> os atlas (the atlases)

o alferes (the lieutenant) -> os alferes (the lieutenants)

o virus(the virus) -> os virus (the viruses)

Nouns ending in –l

Just like nouns which end in –s, the plural formation of nouns ending in –l depends on the location of the stress. Here are the rules for this group of nouns:

Nouns ending in –al

When the stress falls invariably on the last syllable, nouns ending in –al form their plural by dropping –al and replacing it with –ais.

o jornal (the newspaper) -> os jornais (the newspapers)

o material (the material) -> os materiais (the materials)

o general (the general) -> os generais (the generals)

Nouns ending in -el

If the stress falls on the last syllable, nouns which end in –el form their plural by dropping –el and replacing it with –eis. In addition, the plural form is indicated by an acute accent on the last syllable.

o papel (the paper) -> os papéis (the papers)

o hotel (the hotel) -> os hotéis (the hotels)

o pastel (the cake) -> os pasties (the cakes)

When the stress is not on the last syllable, nouns ending in –el form their plural by adding –eis. The acute mark, however, is not placed on the stressed syllable.

o tunnel (the tunnel) -> os túneis (the tunnels)

o telemóvel (the mobile phone) -> os telemóveis (the mobile phones)

Nouns ending in –il

When the stress is on the last syllable, nouns which end in –il drop the –l and add –s to form the plural.

o funil (the funnel) -> os funis (the funnels)

ofuzil (the rifle) -> os fuzis (the rifles)

o canil (the kennel) -> os canis (the kennels)

If the stress is not on the last syllable, nouns which end in –il form their plural by replacing –il with –eis.

o fossil (the fossil) -> os fósseis (the fossils)

o textile (the textile) -> os têxteis (the textiles)

o reptile (the reptile) -> os répteis (the reptiles)

Exceptions:

O mal(the evil) -> os males (the evils)

O consul (the consul) -> os cônsules (the consuls)

57

Nouns which end in −x

If the stress is on the penultimate syllable, the plural form of nouns ending in −x is the same as their singular form.

o tórax (the thorax) -> os thoraxes (the thoraxes)

o clímax (the climax) -> os climax (the climaxes)

Nouns ending in -ão

In most cases, the plural of nouns ending in −ão is formed by replacing −ão with −ões.

o camião (the lorry) -> os camiões (the lorries)

o avião (the airplane) -> os aviões (the airplanes)

o limão (the lemon) -> os limões (the lemons)

The rule also applies to nouns with são or ção endings:

a cancão (the song) -> as cancões (the songs)

a decisão (the decision) -> as decisões (the decisions)

a obrigacão (the obligation) -> as obrigacões (the obligations)

a televiseão (the television) -> as televises (the televisions)

a nacão (the nation) -> as nacões (the nations)

a eleicão (the election) -> as eleicões (the elections)

There are, however, a few nouns with –ão ending that deviate from the above pattern and simply add –s to form their plural. Here is the list:

o irmão (the brother) -> os irmãos (the brothers)

a irmã (the sister) -> as irmãs (the sisters)

cidadão (male the citizen) -> os cidadãos (the male citizens)

a cidadã (the female citizen) -> as cidadãs (the female citizens)

o cristão (the male Christian) -> os cristãos (the female Christian)

a cristã (the male Christian) -> as cristãs (the female Christians)

a mão (the hand) -> as mãos (the hands)

Nouns with –ão ending which are not stressed on the last syllable likewise form the plural with an –s ending.

o sótão (the attic) -> os sótãos (the attics)

o órgão (the organ) -> os órãos (the organs)

o órfão (the orphan) -> os órfãos (the orphans)

Other nouns with –ão ending form their plural by adding –ães:

o escrivão (the scribe) -> os escrivães (the scribes)

o alemão (the German) -> os alemães (the Germans)

o sacristão (the sacristan) -> os sacristães (the sacristans)

o cão (the dog) -> os cães (the dogs)

o capitão (the captain) -> os capitães (captains)

Showing Possession

In English, the possessive is usually expressed by using an apostrophe and "s" ('s) after the noun. Hence, to indicate that a car belongs to Michael, you'll say: Michael's car.

Portuguese nouns have no possessive case. To express possession, you will have to use the preposition "de" which means "of". Hence, to say "Michael's car" in Portuguese, you can use the phrase "o carro de Michael". To be more precise, the ideal translation is "o carro do Michael" or "the car of the Michael". This is an example of how the preposition "de" contracts with the definite article "o" (the) to form "do" (of the).

Most Common Nouns in Portuguese

(the) afternoon	(a) tarde	(ah) tar-deh in EU
(the) afternoon	(a) tarde	(ah) tar-tchee in BR
(the) congratulations	(os) parabéns	(oosh) pah-rah-baingsh
most (of)	a maioria (de)	ah may-oo-ree-ah
the (legal) right	o direito	oo dee-ray-ee-too
the arrival	a chegada	ah shay-gah-dah
the bad luck, the tough	(o) azar	oo ah-zahr
the bad thing	o mal	oo mahll
the balcony, counter	o balcão	oo bahl-kaong
the bath	o banho	oo bah-nyioo
the beginning	o princípio	oo preen-cee-peeoh
the bill	a conta	ah-kong-tah
the bus (Brazil)	o Ônibus	oo oh-nee-booss
the bus (in EU)	o autocarro	oo aoo-toh-car-roo
the card	o cartão	oo cahr-taong
the carefullness	o cuidado	oo-koo-ee-dah-doo
the change	o troco	oo troh-koo
the cold	o frio	oo free-oo
the corner	a esquina	ah sh-keen-ah
the couple	o casal	oo kah-zahl in EU
the couple	o casal	oo kah-zahoo in BR
the day	o dia	oo deer
the door	a porta	ah pohr-tah
the end	o fim	oo feeng

61

English	Portuguese	Pronunciation
the era	a era	ah air-rah
the excuse	a desculpa	ah dsh-cool-pah
the favor	o favor	oo fah-vohr
the first	o primeiro	oo pree-mahee-roh
the flight	o vôo	oo voh-oo
the foot	o pé	oo peh
the fourth, the bedroom	o quarto	oo kwar-too
the front	a frente	ah-frayn-tt EU
the front	a frente	[ah-frayn-tchee] BR
the glass	o copo	oo koh-poo
the go	a ida	ah ee-dah
the help	a ajuda	ah ah-joo-dah
the house, home	a casa	ah kah-sah
the hurry, the ruh	a pressa	ah pray-sah
the journey, trip	a viagem	ah vee-ah-jaying
the last (one)	o Último	oo ool-tee-moo in EU
the last (one)	o Último	oo ool-tchee-moo in BR
the left side	o esquerdo	oo eesh-kayr-doo
the left side	a esquerda	ah eesh-kayr-dah
the luck	a sorte	ah sohr-tt in EU
the luck	a sorte	ah sohr-tchee in BR
the man	o homem	oo oh-mayeen
the message	o recado	oo ray-kah-doo
the minute	o minuto	oo mee-noo-too
the money,	o dinheiro	oo dee-

cash		nyieh-ee-roh
the month	o mês	oo may-sh
the months	os meses	oosh may-say-sh
the name	o nome	oo noh-meh
the news	as novidades	ash noo-vee-dah-desh
the next, the following	o próximo	oo pro-see-moo
the night	a noite	ah noh-ee-
the number	o número	oo noo-may-roh
the people	a gente	ah jayn-tt EU
the people	a gente	ah jayn-tt BR
the people	as pessoas	ash peh-soh-ash
the permission, the license	a licença	ah lee-sayn-sah
the plate, the dish	o prato	oo prah-too
the Portuguese	o português	oo poor-too-gay-sh
the problem	o problema	oh proh-blay-mah
the return, the going back	a volta	ah vohl-tah
the right side	a direita	ah dee-ray-ee-tah
the road, street	a rua	ah roo-ah
the side	o lado	oo lah-doo
the study	o estudo	oo sh-too-doo
the surname	o apelido	oo ah-peh-lee-doo
the thing	a coisa	ah koee-zah
the ticket	o bilhete	oo bee-lyieh-the
the time, hour	a hora	ah oh-rah
the time, the weather	o tempo	oo taym-poo

the timetable	o horário	oo oh-ráh-ree-oo
the traffic light	o semáforo	oo say-mah-foo-roh
the turn, the time	a vez	ah vaysh
the water	a Água	ah ah-goo-ah
the week	a semana	ah say-mah-nah
the wife	a mulher	ah moo-lyier
the woman	a mulher	ah moo-lyier
the word	a palavra	ah pah-lah-vrah
the work, assignment	o trabalho	oo trah-bah-lyioo
the years	os anos	oosh ah-noosh

Chapter 14: Pronouns (Pronomes)

Personal pronouns take the place of nouns and function as subject or object in a sentence or clause.

Subject Pronouns (Pronomes Pessoais)

Portuguese subject pronouns are often omitted in sentences because the verb itself conveys the information needed to identify the subject. For instance, if you say "Falo português", you know that it means "I speak Portuguese" without having to write the pronoun "Eu" (I) at the start of the sentence.

Saying "you" in Portuguese

In English, the pronoun "you" is used to refer to the second person singular and plural. This is almost similar to how the pronouns você (you, singular) and vocês (you, plural) are used in Brazilian Portuguese. The use of "you" in European Portuguese, however, is more complex.

In Portugal, the familiar pronoun "tu" (you, singular) is used when talking to family and friends while the semi-formal form, "você" is used when addressing superior, older people, or people who have no close ties with the speaker.

European Portuguese likewise tend to use the name of the person rather than use the pronoun "you". For instance, instead of telling Francis "Do you watch horror films?" they are more inclined to ask "Does Francis watch horror films?" Likewise, when addressing someone whose name is not known to the speaker, Portuguese are inclined to say "Is the lady okay?" or "Can the Mister help me?".

Here are the Portuguese subject pronouns:

Subject Pronouns	English
eu	I
tu	you (familiar)
você	you (semiformal)
ele	he
ela	she
-	it
nós	we
vocês	you (plural)
eles	they (masculine)
elas	they (feminine)

Since there are only two genders in Portuguese, there is no equivalent pronoun for the English "it".

The pronoun "eles", the masculine form of they, is also used to refer to a group of mixed genders.

Examples:

(Eu) não falo Português.	I don't speak Portuguese.
(Nós) somos dos Estados Unidos.	We are from the United States.
Ela é um grande professor.	She is a great teacher.
Você é um bom amigo.	You are a good friend.
Eles são generosos e carinho.	They are generous and caring.

Direct Object Pronouns

A direct object pronoun receives the action of the verb. In the English sentence "I met him", the pronoun "him" functions as the direct object of the transitive verb "met".

Here are the Portuguese Direct Object Pronouns:

Direct Object Pronouns	English
me	me
te	you (informal)
o	him/it
a	her/it
nos	us
vos/vocês	you (plural)
os	them (masculine)
as	them (feminine)

In European Portuguese, direct object pronouns follow the verb and are separated by a hypen.

Example:

Eu leio o livro. Eu leio-o.

I read the book. I read it.

Direct object pronouns however, must precede the verb when the verb follows the following:

a negative statement

Example:

A criança não o come. -> A child doesn't eat it.

adverbs like "sempre", "também", "já", or "ainda" among others.

Example:

Nós sempre o comemos. We always eat it.

question words like quem, quando, onde, etc.

Example:

Quem lê o livro hoje? -> Who reads the book today?

Quem o lê hoje? -> Who reads it today?

relative pronouns such as "que" (who, which, that, whom), "onde" (where), "quando" (when), etc.

Example:

Ela disse que comeu o pão. She said that she ate the bread.

Ella disse que o comeu. She said she ate it.

Prepositions:

Ela gosta de comer pão com queijo. -> She likes to eat bread with cheese.

Ela gosta de o comer com queijo. -> She likes eating it with cheese.

Chapter 15: Reflexive Pronouns

Reflexive pronouns refer the action back to the subject and are used in sentences where the subject and object are the same. The sentence "I hurt myself" is an example of its use in English where the reflexive pronouns "myself" is also the subject. Reflexive pronouns can stand for the subject pronouns. The reflexive pronoun "se" refers back to the subject pronouns "ele", "ela", "você", "eles", "elas", "vocês", "o senhor", "a senhora", "os senhores" and "as senhoras". They are also exactly parallel to object pronouns.

Reflexive pronouns are commonly used with reflexive verbs which are listed in the dictionary with a –se ending.

Here are the reflexive pronouns:

Subject	Reflexive	English
eu	me	myself
tu (Portugal only)	te	yourself (tu)
ele, ela, você	se	himself, herself, yourself
nós	nos	ourselves
vós (archaic)	vos	yourselves
eles, elas, vocês	se	themselves, yourselves

Possessive Pronouns and Adjectives

Possessive pronouns and adjectives are used to express ownership. Possessive describe, replace or accompany a noun. Possessive pronouns and adjectives are identical. Possesive adjectives are placed before the noun they modify while possessive pronouns replace a noun and are preceded by a definite article. Both must agree in number and gender with the object possessed and not with the possessor.

Examples:

Meu carro é caro.	My car is expensive.
Minhas casas são grande.	My houses are big.
O carro é o **meu**.	The car is mine.

Possessor	Possessed object			
	Masculine		Feminine	
	Singular	Plural	Singular	Plural
eu	meu	meus	minha	minhas
tu	teu	teus	tua	tuas
ele, ela, você	seu	seus	sua	suas
nós	nosso	nossos	nossa	nossas
vós	vosso	vossos	vossa	vossas
eles, elas, vocês	seu	seus	sua	suas

Demonstrative Pronouns and Demonstrative Adjectives

Demonstrative words indicate the distance between the speaker and another noun or pronoun. They correspond to the English words "this", "these", "that", and "those".

Here are the **demonstrative pronouns:**

isto	this
istos	these
isso	that
issos	those
aquilo	that (over there)
aquilos	those (over there)

Examples:

O que é isso? -> What is that?

Estes são meus. -> These are mine.

Demonstrative adjectives

Demonstrative adjectives are used to modify nouns. You use them to express "this house" or "those books". Demonstrative adjectives must match the gender and number of the noun they modify.

Demonstrative Adjectives

Masculine	Feminine	English
este	esta	this
estes	estas	these
esse	esse	that
esses	essas	those
aquele	aquela	that (over there)
aqueles	aquelas	those (over there

Examples:

Estes carros são caros.	These cars are expensive.
Essas casas são grandes e bela.	Those houses are big and beautiful.

Interrogative Pronouns

Interrogative pronouns are words you use when asking questions. They correspond to the English words "who", "what", "when", "where", "which", "how", and "why".

Here are the interrogative pronouns in Portuguese:

quem?	who
quens?	who (plural)
que...?	what
quando?	when
por que...?	why
onde?	where
como?	how
qual?	which
quanto?	how much

When asking about two or more persons, you use the plural form "quens", instead of "quem" (who). For example, "Quem são essas pessoas?" (Who are those people?)

The pronoun "onde" (where) is commonly used with the prepositions "a" (to) and "de" (of/from). It contracts when used with "a" into "aonde" which means "to/at where".

It is used to indicate direction or location. For instance, to express "to where are you going?", you'll say "Aonde você vai?".

The pronoun "que" (what) is commonly used with the article "o" as a matter of practice. There is no difference in meaning whether you use "o" or not. For example, "o que dizem" means the same things as "o que dizem" (What are they saying?)

To ask "why?" as a single-word question, you'll say "(o) por quê?"

Chapter 16: Adjectives (Adjetivos)

An adjective modify or describe a noun or a pronoun. Adjectives can be masculine or feminine and singular or plural depending on the gender or number of the noun they modify.

Adjectives commonly end in –o, -e, or a consonant.

When an adjective ends in –o, it can have four different forms:

caro (expensive)

	singular	plural
masculine	caro	caros
feminine	cara	caras

The masculine noun brinquedo (toy) can be described as "um brinquedo caro" (an expensive toy") or "brinquedos caros"(expensive toys). To describe the feminine noun casa (house), you can say "uma casa cara" (an expensive house) or "casas caras" (expensive houses).

Adjectives ending in –e can have two forms, having similar forms for the masculine and the feminine and in the plural.

forte (strong)

	singular	plural
masculine	forte	fortes
feminine	forte	fortes

The noun homem (man) may thus be described as "um forte homem" (a strong man) or "os homens fortes" (the strong men). On the other hand, a mulher (woman) can be described as "a mulher forte" (the strong woman) or "mulheres fortes" (strong women).

Other Examples:

Este é um carro caro. (This is an expensive car.)

Ele é um homem humilde. (He is a humble man.)

Foi mais uma semana produtiva. (It was another productive week.)

Minha mãe é uma mulher carinhosa e amorosa. (My mother is a caring and loving woman.)

Foi mais uma semana produtiva. (It was another productive week.)

Minha mãe é uma mulher carinhosa e amorosa. (My mother is a caring and loving woman.)

In general, Portuguese adjectives come after the noun. There are, however, some exceptions. For instance, the irregular adjectives mau (bad) and bom (good) are nearly always placed before the noun. The adjective "grande" can take on a different meaning when placed before or after a noun. When it comes before the noun, "grande" means "great" but when placed after it, it means big or large. When placed before a noun, the adjective"bom" (good) ascribes good inner qualities to the noun being described while it means good-hearted when placed after it. Some adjectives may also be placed before the noun for style or emphasis.

Irregular Adjectives

Irregular adjectives have distinct forms to express the gender and number.

Adjectives with –m ending have similar forms for the masculine and feminine genders in both singular and plural. In addition, they change to –n before adding "s" to form the plural.

jovem (young)

	singular	plural
masculine	jovem	jovens
feminine	jovem	jovens

On the other hand, the adjective "ruin" (bad) has four distinct forms:

	singular	plural
masculine	ruim	ruins
feminine	ruina	ruinas

Likewise, the adjective "bom" (good) has four separate forms:

	singular	plural
masculine	bom	bons
feminine	boa	boas

Adjectives ending in -ão generally have four separate forms.

são (healthy/sane)

	singular	plural
masculine	são	sãos
feminine	sã	sãs

Past Participles as Adjectives

Adjectives derived from past participles are generally used in the passive voice.

As a verb, past participles have only one form. When used as an adjective, past participles take four distinct forms.

Endings of adjectives formed from past participles of –ar verbs

	singular	plural
masculine	-ado	-ados
feminine	-ada	-adas

Endings of adjectives formed from past participles of –er and –ir verbs

	singular	plural
masculine	-ido	-idos
feminine	-ida	-idas

Comparatives and Superlatives

In English, the comparative is formed by either adding –er to the ending of an adjective or by placing a modifier before the adjective. The superlative, on the other hand, is formed by adding –est to the adjective or placing a modifier before the adjective. Thus, small becomes smaller in the comparative and smallest in the superlative.

In Portuguese, the comparative is formed by using the following phrases:

tão+adjective+como -> as+adjective+as

mais+adjective+(do)que -> ____ - er than

Examples:

Marco é tão alto como Jeffrey.	Marco is as tall as Jeffrey.
Ricardo é mais alto do que Marco.	Ricardo is taller than Marco.
Regina é tão alta como Ricardo.	Regina is as tall as Ricardo.

To express the superlative, you have to use a definite article before "mais" and the adjective to mean that the noun being described is "the most ____".

Examples:

Arturo é o mais alto.	Arturo is the tallest.
Carlota é o mais alta.	Carlota is the tallest.
Estes meninos são os mais altos.	These boys are the tallest.

Another way to emphasize a noun's quality without resorting to comparison is by using the word "muito" (very) or by adding the –íssimo ending. Take note that –íssimo also has four distinct forms: -íssimo, -íssima, -íssimos, and -íssimas.

Examples:

Cara é muito grande.	Cara is very big.
Cara é grandissima!	Cara is so big!
Renaldo é muito alto.	Renaldo is very tall.
Renaldo é altissimo!	Renaldo is so tall!

Irregular Comparative and Superlative Forms

There are several adjectives with irregular forms in the superlative and comparative. Some of the adjectives have both regular and irregular forms. The regular forms are used to describe physical qualities while the irregular forms are used for abstract descriptions.

adjective	comparative	superlative
bom(good)	melhor(better)	o melhor(the best)
mau(bad)	pior(worse)	o pior(the worst)
muito(much, many)	mais(more)	o mais(the most)
pouco(a few/a little)	menos(less)	o menos(the least)
alto(tall/high)	mais alto(taller/higher)	o mais alto the tallest, higher
alto(tall/high)	superior(higher)	o supremo(the highest)
baixo (short/low)	mais baixo (shorter/lower)	o mais baixo (the shortest, lowest)
baixo (short/low)	inferior(lower)	o ínfimo(the lowest)
grande (big/great)	mais grande(bigger/greater)	o mais grande(the biggest/greatest)
grande (big/great)	maior(bigger/older)	o maior(the biggest/oldest)
pequeno(little/small)	mais pequeno(smaller)	o mais pequeno(the smallest)
pequeno(little/small)	menor(smaller/younger)	o menor(the smallest/youngest)

Most Commonly Used Portuguese Adjectives

(the) worse	(o)pior/(os) piores	(oo) pee-ohr
open	aberto	ah-bayr-too
tall	alto	ahl-tooEU/ahoo-to BR
small (short in height)	baixo	bah-ee-shoo
cheap	barato	bah-rah-too
good	bom/boa/bons/boas	bong
pretty, beautiful	bonito	boo-nee-too
expensive, dear	caro	kah-roo
married	casado	kah-zah-doo
long (in lengh)	comprido	coom-pree-doo
short (in lengh)	curto	coor-too
direct	directo	dee-reh-too
(legal) right	direito	dee-ray-too
right (hand), straight	direito	dee-ray-too
left hand	esquerdo	eesh-kehr-doo
closed	fechado	fay-shah-doo
ugly	feio	fay-eeoo
cold	frio	free-oo
big, large	grande/grandes	gran-deh EU/gran-chee BR
long	longa	lon-gah
far (from)	longe (de)	lon-gee
fully booked (e.g. hotel)	lotado	loo-tah-doo
packed with people	lotado	loo-tah-doo

83

bad	mau/má/maus/más	maaooh
better	melhor/melhores	may-lyiohr
new, young	novo	noh-voo
small, short	pequeno	pay-kay-noo
near, close (to)	perto (de)	pehr-too
hot, warm	quente	kayn-the EU/kayn-chee BR
serious, honest	sério	say-ree-oo
old	velho	vay-lyioo

Chapter 17: Verbs (Verbos)

Verbs express action or state of being. In addition, Portuguese verbs identify the doer of the action by taking appropriate endings to reflect the gender and number of the subject.

Almost all verbs are regular and they conform to the endings of the three major verb categories: the –ar verbs, -er verbs, and –ir verbs. The verb groups are named after their ending in the infinitive. Because 99.99% of verbs fall under these groups, you can confidently conjugate verbs by simply memorizing 5 ending for 5 different subjects.

Verb Moods

Portuguese verbs have 4 moods:

Indicative -> The indicative mood is the most basic mood. It expresses action that happens in the present, will happen in the future, and have occurred in the past. It is also the mood you use when asking questions.

Imperative -> The imperative mood indicates command or orders.

Conditional -> The conditional mood expresses the possibility for something to happen under certain conditions

Subjunctive -> The subjunctive mood expresses a surreal action that may or may not happen

Verb Tenses

Tenses specify the time when an action takes place. Portuguese verbs have different tenses under each mood

The Indicative Mood Tenses

The indicative mood has 8 tenses:

Present tense -> Eu como. (I eat)

Present continuous -> Eu estou comendo. (I am eating.)

Perfect past -> Eu tenho comido. (I have eaten.)

Imperfect past -> Eu comia. (I was eating.)

Near future -> Eu vou comer. (I'm going to eat)

Perfect past -> Eu tenho comido. (I have eaten.)

Imperfect past -> Eu tinha comido. (I had eaten.)

Far future -> Eu comerei. (I will eat.)

The perfect past and the imperfect past tense are compound verbs using the conjugated forms of the verb Ter+main verb.

Imperative Mood

Since the imperative mood expresses command, there are no tenses but verbs are categorized into the following:

Positive state -> expresses positive command

Example: Vá à biblioteca. (Go to the library.)

Negative state -> expresses negative command

Example: -> Não vá para a biblioteca. (Don't go to the library.)

Subjunctive Mood

The subjuctive mood expresses wishes, probability, and actions that are not likely to happen.

Subjunctive verbs are easy to identify because they are always used after expressions lke these:

espero que(I hope that) _____

Deus queira quem(God wishes that) _____

talves (maybe) _____

Here are the verb tenses under the subjunctive mood:

Present tense

Example:

Talvez eu esteja triste. -> Maybe I'm sad.

Imperfect past tense

Example:

Se eu estivesse satisfeito ___ (If I were satisfied)

Future tense

Example:

Quando eu for satisfeito ___ (When I'm satisfied ___)

Conjugating Verbs

To conjugate a verb, you only need to drop the –ar, -er, or –ir ending to get the verb stem then add the appropriate personal endings.

The verb comer, for example, is an –er verb based on its ending in the infinitive. To conjugate comer, you will first have to get the stem which is "com" then add the ending that coincides with the subject. If the subject is Eu (I), then the ending should be –o and the conjugated verb is "como", which means "I eat."

The Present Indicative Tense (Presente)

The present tense shows action that happens in and around the present time.

Here is the conjugation table for the present indicative tense

Subject	English	-ar verbs	-er verbs	-ir verbs
eu	I	-o	-o	-o
tu (Portugal only)	you (informal)	-as	-es	-es
ele, ela, você	he, she, you (formal)	-a	-e	-e
nós	we	-amos	-emos	-imos
vós (archaic)	you (informal)	-ais	-eis	-is
eles, elas, vocês	he, she, you (formal, pl)	-am	-em	-em

The conjugation table for the verbs ajudar (to help), escrever (to write) and partir (to leave) in the present indicative tense will be:

Subject	(ajudar)	(escrever)	(partir)
eu	ajudo	escrevo	parto
tu (Portugal only)	ajudas	escreves	partes
ele, ela, você	ajuda	escreve	parte
nós	ajudamos	escrevemos	partimos
vós (archaic)	ajudais	escreveis	partris
eles, elas, vocês	ajudam	escrevem	partem

Examples:

(Eu) escrevo o canção. -> I write the songs.

Eu ajudo a minha mãe cozinhar. -> I help my mother cook.

The Preterit or Past Indicative (Pretérito perfeito)

The past tense shows an action that happened in the past.

Here is the conjugation table for the past tense:

Subject	English	-ar verbs	-er verbs	-ir verbs
eu	I	-ei	-i	-i
tu (Portugal)	you (informal)	-ste	-este	-iste
ele, ela, você	he, she, you (formal)	-ou	-eu	-iu
nós	we	-ámos	-emos	-imos
vós (archaic)	you (informal)	-astes	-estes	-istes
eles, elas, vocês	he, she, you (formal, pl)	-aram	-eram	-iram

The conjugation table for the verbs ajudar (to help), escrever (to write) and partir (to leave) in the simple past tense will be:

Subject	ajudar	escrever	partir
eu	ajudei	escreveri	parti
tu (Portugal)	ajudste	escreveste	partiste
ele, ela, você	ajudou	escreveu	partiu
nós	ajudámos	escrevemos	partimos
vós (archaic)	ajudastes	escrevestes	partistes
eles, elas, vocês	ajudaram	escreveram	partiram

A criança ganhou o concurso. -> The child won the contest.

Eu abri a porta para ele. -> I opened the door for him.

Eu enviei meu relatório ontem. -> I submitted my report yesterday.

The Imperfect Indicative Tense (Pretérito imperfeito)

The imperfect tense is used for expressing an event that was occuring at a certain moment in time. The English sentence "I was reading a book" describes something that was happening at a particular time. The imperfect tense is often used to set the sentence for the use of the perfect tense: "I was reading a book when the doorbell rang."

Here is the conjgugation table for the imperfect indicative mood:

Subject	English	-ar verbs	-er verbs	-ir verbs
eu	I	-ava	-ia	-ia
tu (Portugal)	you (informal)	-avas	-ias	-ias
ele, ela, você	he, she, you (formal)	-ava	-ia	-ia
nós	we	-ávamos	-íamos	-íamos
vós (archaic)	you (informal)	-áveis	-íeis	-íeis
eles, elas, vocês	he, she, you (formal, pl)	-avam	-iam	-iam

Here is the conjugation table for the verbs ajudar (to help), escrever (to write) and partir (to leave) in the imperfect indicative tense:

Subject	(ajudar)	(escrever)	(abrir)
eu	ajudava	escrevia	abria
tu (Portugal)	ajudavas	escrevias	abrias
ele, ela, você	ajudava	escrevia	abria
nós	ajudávamos	escrevíamos	abríamos
vós (archaic)	ajudáveis	escrevíeis	abríeis
eles, elas, vocês	ajudavam	escreviam	abriam

Examples:

(Eu) escrevia quando você chegou. -> I was writing when you arrived.

Tu fal avas. -> You were speaking.

The Future Indicative Tense (Futuro)

The future tense expresses an action that will happen in the future.

Here is the verb table for the Future tense:

Subject	English	-ar verbs	-er verbs	-ir verbs
eu	I	-arei	-crei	-irei
tu (Portugal only)	you (informal)	-arás	-erás	-irás
ele, ela, você	he, she, you (formal)	-ará	-erá	-irá
nós	we	-aremos	-eremos	-iremos
vós (archaic)	you (informal)	-areis	-ereis	-ireis
eles, elas, vocês	he, she, you (formal, pl)	-arão	-erão	-irão

Here is how to conjugate the verbs ajudar, escrever, and partir in the future tense:

Subject	(ajudar)	(escrever)	(abrir)
eu	ajudarei	escreverei	escrivirei
tu (Portugal only)	ajudarás	escreverás	escrivirás
ele, ela, você	ajudará	escreverá	escrivirá
nós	ajudaremos	escreveremos	escriviremos
vós (archaic)	ajudareis	escrevereis	escrivireis
eles, elas, vocês	ajudarão	escreverão	escrivirão

Eu ajudarei minha mãe. -> I'll help my mother.

Eu comerei bolo de banana amanhã. -> I will eat banana cake tomorrow.

The Conditional Mood

The conditional tense expresses actions that would happen. It is used mainly in hypothetical statements. The English phrase "I would write your speech but I can't" is an example of a conditional statement and the verb "I would" is in the conditional mood.

Here is the conjugation table for the conditional mood/tense:

Subject	English	-ar verbs	-er verbs	-ir verbs
eu	I	-aria	-eria	-iria
tu (Portugal only)	you (informal)	-arias	-erias	-irias
ele, ela, você	he, she, you (formal)	-aria	-eria	-iria
nós	we	-aríamos	-eríamos	-iríamos
vós (archaic)	you (informal)	-aríeis	-eríeis	-iríeis
eles, elas, vocês	he, she, you (formal, pl)	-ariam	-eriam	-iriam

Here is how you will conjugate the verbs ajudar, escrever, and partir in the conditional:

Subject	ajudar	escrever	partir
eu	ajudaria	escreveria	partiria
tu (Portugal only)	ajudarias	escreverias	partirias
ele, ela, você	ajudaria	escreveria	partiria
nós	ajudaríamos	escreveríamos	partiríamos
vós (archaic)	ajudaríeis	escreveríeis	partiríeis
eles, elas, vocês	ajudariam	escreveriam	partiriam

Eu lo ajudaria mas estou ocupado. -> I would help him but I'm busy.

The Imperative Mood and Tense

The imperative mood is used when expressing commands. There is no verb form for the subjects I, he, she, or they in the imperative because commands are directed to the second person. European Portuguese uses the verbs forms for "tu" to express commands except when a negative command is expressed as in the case of "não partas" (don't leave) or "não vendas" (don't sell).

Here is the conjugation table for verbs in the imperative mood:

Subject	English	-ar verbs	-er verbs	-ir verbs
tu (Portugal)	you (informal)	-a	-e	-e
você	you (formal)	-e	-a	-a
nós	we	-emos	-amos	-amos
vós (archaic)	you (informal,	-ai	-ei	-i

	pl)			
vocês	you (formal,pl)	-em	-am	-am

Here's how you will conjugate the verbs ajudar, escrever, and partir in the imperative:

Subject	ajudar	escrever	partir
tu (Portugal)	ajuda	escreve	parte
você	ajude	escreva	parta
nós	ajudemos	escrevamos	partamos
vós (archaic)	ajudai	escrevei	parti
vocês	ajudem	escrevam	partam

Examples:

Me deixa em paz!	Leave me alone!
Deixa o quarto agora!	Leave the room now!
Vá para cama, agora!	Go to bed now!

The Present Progressive

The present progressive tense is equivalent to the English construction "to be + _ing" or "I am studying". To express the present progressive which is a compound verb, you will use the verb estar (to be) with a verb in the present participle.

Take note that the present participle is invariable and the endings for the three groups of verbs are as follows:

-ar verbs (ajudar)	-er verbs (escrever)	-ir verbs (partir)
-ando (ajudando)	-endo (escrevendo)	-indo (partindo)

Here is the present indicative tense of the verb estar:

Subject	English	estar
eu	I	estou
tu (Port.)	you (informal)	estás
ele, ela, você	he, she, you (formal)	está
nós	we	estamos
vós (archaic)	you (informal)	estais
eles, elas, vocês	he, she, you (formal, pl)	estão

To say:

I am writing.	(Eu) estou escrevendo.
He is helping.	Ele está ajudando.
You are writing.	Tu estás escrevendo.
We are helping.	Nos estamos ajudando.

97

The Past Participle

The past participle is used in forming compound verb constructions and corresponds to English verbs ending in –ed. Verbs in past participle form can also be used as adjectives just like their English counterpart. Just like regular adjectives, they must vary to agree with the gender and number of the noun they describe.

Here is the conjugation table for the verbs ajudar (to help), escrever (to write), and partir (to leave) in the past participle.

-ar verbs (ajudar)	-er verbs (escrever)	-ir verbs (partir)
-ado (ajudado)	-ido (escrevido)	-ido (partido)

The past participle is used with the verb ter (to have) to form a compound verb.

Some verbs are irregular in the past participle including the following verbs:

vir	to come	vindo	come
cobrir	to cover	coberto	covered
morrer	to die	morto	died
fazer	to do	feito	done
abrir	to open	aberto	opened
pôr	to put	posto	placed
dizer	to say	dito	said
ver	to see	visto	seen
escrever	to write	escrito	written

Some past participles are irregular when used as adjectives but are regular when used as verb:

5Infinitive	Adjective		Past Participle	
aceitar (to accept)	aceito	accepted	aceitado	accepted
nascer (to be born)	nato	born	nascido	born
limpar (to clean)	limpo	clean	limpado	cleaned
fritar (to fry)	frito	fried	fritado	fried
juntar (to join)	junto	together	juntado	joined
acender (to light)	aceso	lit	acendido	lit
pagar (to pay)	pago	paid	pagado	paid
gastar (to spend)	gasto	spent	gastado	spent
ganhar (to win)	ganho	won	ganhado	won

Examples of past participles used as adjective:

o tempo **perdido**	the wasted time
o frango **frito**	the fried chicken
o jogo **ganho**	the won game
a conta **paga**	the paid bill

Compound Verbs

A compound verb is a combination of two or more verbs involving the verb "ter" + the past participle form. This compound can be used in many moods and tenses. It is most commonly used in the present indicative to mean "I have+ past participle", in the imperfect tense to indicate "I had+past participle", in the future indicative to express "I will have+past participle", and in the conditional to indicate "I would have+past participle".

The verb "ter" is an irregular verb and has the following conjugations in the different tenses:

	Indicative Mood					
Subject	Present	Preterit	Imperfect	Future	Conditional	Imperative
eu	tenho	tive	tinha	terei	teria	
Tu (Portugal)	tens	tiveste	tinhas	terás	terias	tem
ele, ela, você	tem	teve	tinha	terá	teria	tenha
nós	temos	tivemos	tínhamos	teremos	teríamos	tenhamos
vós (archaic)	tendes	tivestes	tínheis	tereis	teríeis	tende
eles, elas, vocês	têm	tiveram	tinham	terão	teriam	tenham

	Subjunctive Mood		
Subject	Present	Imperfect	Future
eu	tenha	tivesse	tiver
tu (Portugal)	tenhas	tivesses	tiveres
ele, ela, você	tenha	tivesse	tiver
nós	tenhamos	tivéssemos	tivermos
vós (archaic)	tenhais	tivésseis	tiverdes
eles, elas, vocês	tenham	tivessem	tiverem

Participle Forms	
Present Participle	Past Participle
tendo	tido

To use "ter" with the verb estudar (to study) in the different tenses, you will have the following compound constructions:

Present Indicative	I have studied	Eu tenho estudado.
Imperfect Tense	I had studied.	Eu tinha estudado.
Future Indicative	I will have studied.	Eu terei estudiado.
Conditional	I would have studied.	Eu teria estudiado.

Reflexive Verbs

Reflexive verbs indicate that the doer (subject) of the action is also the receiver of the action (object). Reflexive verbs are accompanied by reflexive pronouns and are listed in the dictionary with the –se ending, the reflexive pronoun for the third person. They are conjugated in the same way that regular verbs are conjugated except that they end with a hypen and the reflexive pronoun –se. The pronoun may also be placed before the verb.

Examples:

Como você se chama? -> How are you called? /What is your name?

Eu lavo-me. -> I wash myself.

Here are common reflexive verbs:

Reflexive Verb	Literal Translation	English
cortar-se	to cut oneself	to cut
deitar-se	to go to sleep, to retire	to lie down
enxugar-se	to dry oneself	to dry off
lavar-se	to wash onself	to wash up
lembrar-se	to remind oneself	to remember
levantar-se	to get oneself up	to get up
machucar-se	to hurt oneself	to bruise
pentear-se	to brush, comb oneself	to comb
sentar-se	to sit oneself down	to sit down
sentir-se	to feel oneself	to feel
servir-se	to help oneself	to help oneself
vestir-se	to put on clothes, to dress oneself	to dress
vestir-se	to dress oneself	to dress

The Verbs Ser, Estar, and Ficar

The verbs ser, estar, and ficar all translate to the English verb "to be" but have distinct uses.

Ser (to be)

The verb ser is used to indicate long term or permanent characteristics or conditions. It is used to associate people with their occupation when used with a noun. It is also the verb used for telling the time of day, a recurring event.

Ele é uma pessoa inteligente.	He is an intelligent person.
Ela é uma mulher generosa.	She is a generous woman.
Nós somos empregados.	We are employees.
Eles são estudantes.	They are students.
São três horas.	It's three o'clock.
É meio-dia.	It's noon.

Verb Table for Ser

Subject	Present	Perfect Past	Imperfect Past	Futuro
eu	sou	fui	era	seria
tu (Port.)	és	foste	eras	serás
ele, ela, você	é	foi	era	será
nós	somos	fomos	éramos	seremos
vós (archaic)	sois	fostes	éreis	sereis
eles, elas, vocês	são	foram	eram	serão

103

Estar (to be)

The verb estar is used to indicate temporary characteristics, conditions, or state of being. It indicates a temporary quality if used with an adjective. It is used when talking about the weather.

Está nublado.	It is cloudy.
Está chovendo.	It is rainy.
Estamos felizes.	We are happy.
Ele está doente.	He is sick.

Verb Table for estar

Subject	Present	Perfect Past	Imperfect Past	Futuro
eu	estou	estive	estava	estarei
tu (Port.)	estás	estiveste	estavas	estarás
ele, ela, você	está	esteve	estava	estará
nós	estamos	estivemos	estávamos	estaremos
vós (archaic)	estais	estivestes	estáveis	estareis
eles, elas, vocês	estão	estiveram	estavam	estarão

Ficar (to be, to be located, to stay)

The verb ficar means to be located but it expresses the verb "to be" and can be used as an alternative to ser and estar when talking about locations.

O museu fica aqui. -> The museum is here.

Ela fica na rua. -> She is in the street.

Verb table for ficar

Subject	Present	Perfect Past	Imperfect Past	Futuro
eu	fico	fiquei	ficava	ficarei
tu (Port.)	ficas	ficaste	ficavas	ficarás
ele, ela, você	fica	ficou	ficava	ficará
nós	ficamos	ficámos/ficamos	ficávamos	ficaremos
vós (archaic)	ficais	ficastes	ficáveis	ficareis
eles, elas, vocês	ficam	ficaram	ficavam	ficarão

The Passive Voice

The passive voice is a sentence construction where the object in the active voice becomes the subject. There are two ways of forming the passive voice in Portuguese.

The most common passive construction is the use of the reflexive pronoun "se" with the verb which translates to a general subject:

Os gatos se limpam. -> The cats clean themselves.

Another way to form the passive is by using the verb "ser" with the past participle. When constructing passive sentences with "ser", the past participles function as adjectives which must vary in form to match the noun's gender and number.

As casas são construídas. -> The houses are built.

As cortinas são costurados. -> The curtains are sewn.

Most Commonly Used Verbs

can, to be able to	poder	poh-dehr
to answer	responder	raysh-pohn-dehr
to arrive	chegar	shay-garh
to ask (for something)	pedir	peh-deer EU/pee-cheer BR
to ask (questions)	perguntar	pehr-goon-tahr
to be (permanent)	ser	sayhr
to be (temporary)	estar	eesh-tahr
to be located, to stay, become	ficar	fee-kahr
to bring	trazer	trah-zehr
to change, exchange	trocar	tro-kahr
to climb, go up	subir	soo-beehr
to close	fechar	fay-shahr
to come	vir	veerr
to come back, do again	voltar (a+other verb)	vohl-tahr ah
to do, to make	fazer	fah-zayhr
to feel	sentir	sayn-teehr EU/sayn-cheehr BR
to fly	voar	voo-ahr
to forgive	desculpar-se	daysh-cool-parr say
to go	ir	eerh
to go down, descend	descer	desh-sayrh
to have (to)	ter (de)	tay-rh (deh) EU
to have (to)	ter (de)	tay-rh (chee) BR
to help	ajudar	ah-joo-darh
to improve, to better	melhorar	may-lyio-rahr

107

to keep, stay with	ficar com	fee-kahr con
to know (skills)	saber	sah-behr
to learn	aprender	ah-prayn-dayrh
to leave behind, to let	deixar (de)	day-sharh
to leave, go out	sair	sah-eehr
to like	gostar de	goosh-tahr
to live	morar	moh-rahr
to look (at)	olhar	oh-lyiahr
to need	precisar	pray-cee-zahr
to open	abrir	ah-breer
to prefer	preferir	pray-fay-reehr
to put	pôr	pohr
to read	ler	layrh
to say, tell	dizer	dee-zayhr EU
to say, tell	dizer	tchee-zayhr BR
to say, to tell (Brazil)	falar	fah-lahr
to see, watch	ver	vayrr
to seem, to look like	parecer	pah-ray-cehr
to sign	assinar	ah-see-narh
to sit down	sentar(-se)	sayn-tahr
to sleep	dormir	door-meer
to speak	falar	fah-lahr
to study	estudar	ees-too-dahr
to take, get, catch	apanhar	ah-pah-nyiarh
to think, guess, find.	achar	ah-shahr
to travel, commute	viajar	vee-ah-jar
to understand	perceber [EU]	payr-seh-behr
to use	usar	oo-sahr
to walk, to be doing something	andar	an-darh

to work	trabalhar	trah-bah-lyiahr
to write, spell	escrever	aysh-cray-vehr

Chapter 18: Adverbs (Advérbios)

Portuguese adverbs are invariable words that modify a verb, an adjective, and another adverb. They can be placed before or after the verb they modify.

Many adverbs end in –mente which is the equivalent of –ly in English. These adverbs are formed by adding –mente to the feminine form of the adjective. For instance, the feminine form of the adjective lento (slow) is lenta. To form the adverb, just add –mente to lenta: lenta + mente = lentamente (slowly).

Portuguese uses different forms and context of adverbs to indicate time, place, quantity, intensity, mode, affirmation, doubt, denial, and exclusivity. Besides one- word adverbs, there are the so-called adverbial phrases or adverbial locutions.

Here are the most common Portuguese adverbs:

Adverbs of Time

Portuguese	English
hoje	today
amanhã	tomorrow
ontem	yesterday
cedo	early
já não	not any more
agora	now nowadays
já	now already
tarde	late
então	then so

sempre	always constantly all the time
logo	immediately immediately after shortly shortly later
nunca	ever never
primeiro	firstly first of all
ainda	still yet
antes	before
dantes	formerly those times before
enfim	anyway
antigamente	formerly those times before

Take note that the adverb "sempre" always comes after the verb.

Examples:

Ela sempre vem na hora certa.	She always comes on time.
Nós jogou tênis ontem.	We played tennis yesterday.
Ela nunca vai mentir para mim.	She will never lie to me.

Adverbs of Place

Portuguese	English
aqui	here
cá	here
lá	over there
alí	over there
aí	there
	then (Brazilian Portuguese)
perto (de)	near
	next to
	around the corner
dentro (de)	inside
longe (de)	far from
fora (de)	outside
atrás (de)	behind
	at the rear
adiante (de)	ahead
acima	above
detrás (de)	behind
debaixo	under
	underneath
abaixo	below

Examples:

Sua secretária caminhou atrás dela. -> Her secretary walked behind her.

O gato está jogando debaixo da mesa. -> The cat is playing under the table.

Ela está aqui. -> She's here.

Adverbs indicating manner or mode:

Portuguese	English
bem	well
melhor	better
mal	badly
pior	worse
devagar	slowly
depressa	quickly
assim	so, therefore this way
como	as, like the way like
sobretudo	above all
efetivamente	actually
facilmente	easily
principalmente	mainly
rapidamente	quickly

Examples:

O menino se sente bem. -> The boy feels well.

A velha caminhou lentamente. -> The old woman walked slowly.

Ele saiu rapidamente. -> He left quickly.

Adverbs indicating intensity or quantity

Portuguese	English
mais	more, plus
pouco	little
muito	very, much, too, too much
menos	less, minus
quanto (de)	as much
tão (de)	so much
tanto	as much, too much
quase (de)	almost
demsiado (de)	too much
bastante	enough, a lot, too much

O criminoso foi quase pego pelo policial.

(The criminal was almost caught by the police officer.)

Minha filha está mais animado do que nunca. (My daughter is more excited than ever.)

Adverbs indicating affirmation

Portuguese	English
sim	yes
decerto	certainly
certamente	certainly, for sure
realmente	really

Ele é realmente generoso. (He is really generous.)

Ele certamente está deixando. (He is certainly leaving.)

Adverbs indicating denial:

Portuguese	English
nunca	never, ever
jamais	never ever
não	no, don't
nem	neither, nor

Eu nunca vou deixar a minha mãe. (I will never leave my mother.)

Não se esqueça de fazer sua lição de casa. (Don't forget to do your homework.)

Adverbs indicating doubt

Portuguese	English
provavelmente	probably
talvez	may, maybe, perhaps
se calhar	may, maybe, perhaps

115

Provavelmente, vou dormir com mais freqüência. (I will probably sleep more.)

Adverbs indicating exclusivity

Portuguese	English
apenas	only, just
só	only, just
unicamente	only, just
somente	only, just
senão	otherwise

Ele só quer o melhor para seus filhos. (He only wants the best for his children.)

Ele está apenas pensando em sua família. (He is just thinking about his family.)

Adverbial Phrases

Portuguese	English
às direitas	right, well
às escuras	in the dark
às vezes	sometimes
em breve	soon, shortly
ao acaso	randomly
em vão	in vain
de baixo	under
por acaso	by chance
à toa	crazily
a sós	alone
de lado	beside
com efeito	effectively
em resumo	in conclusion
de novo	again, one more time
a cada passo	often
de vez em quando	now and then from time to time once in a blue moon
à vontade	comfortably
por alto	roughly
actualmente	nowadays
com certeza	surely, certainly
de facto (EP)	actually
de fato (BR)	actually
como deve ser	properly

Ele lutou **em vão**. (He fought back in vain.)

Ele descobriu a verdade **por acaso**. (He found out the truth by chance.)

Ele seguirá **em breve**. (He will follow shortly.)

Meu pai iria visitar **de vez em quando**. (My father would visit once in a while.)

Chapter 19: Prepositions (Preposições)

Prepositions connect words within a sentence or phrase. They are the equivalent of on, in, to, about, at, with, of, or around. Portuguese prepositions always precede the noun.

Here are the most common prepositions:

Prepositions of location

à	at
em	in, on, at
perto (de)	near
ao longo(de)	along
atrás (de)	behind
ao lado(de)	next (to)
em redor(de)	around
acima (de)/por cima(de)	above
entre	(in) between
debaixo (de)	below, under
à frente(de)	in front of
dentro (de)	in, inside
em frente(de)	in front (of)
fora (de)	outside (of)

em cima(de)	on top (of)
no meio(de)	in the middle(of), in the center(of)

Vamos estudar na biblioteca esta tarde. (We will study at the library this afternoon).

Meu filho fica **entre** a professora eo diretor . (My son stands between his teacher and the school director.)

Ele dirigiu **ao redor do** parquet. (He drove around the park.)

Ele ficou **atrás de** seu amigo. (He stood behind his friend.)

Ele pulou **sobre** o penhasco. (He jumped over the cliff.)

O cão está jogando **debaixo da** mesa. (The dog is playing under the table.)

Ela pratica seu discurso **na frente do** espelho. (She practices her speech in front of the mirror.)

Prepositions of direction

a	to
de	from
através (de)	through
sobre	over
para	for, to

Ele viajou **da** Europa **para** a Ásia. -> (He travelled from Europe to Asia.)

Ele veio **de** Nova Iorque. -> (He came from New York.)

Prepositions of Time

antes (de)	before
dentro (de)	in
depois (de)	after
desde	since
durante	during, for
entre	between
até	until
em + months	in + months
em + year	in + year
em + day	onthe+day+month/ on+month+day

Vou chamá-lo **antes d**e 7 horas da noite. (I will call you before 7 o'clock tonight.)

Eu não o vejo **desde** sexta-feira. (I haven't seen him since Friday.)

Vou encontrá-lo **entre** 7 e 11 amanhã de manhã. (I will meet you between 7 and 11 tomorrow morning.)

Nasci **em** 1992. (I was born in 1992).

Meu aniversário é **em** 1 de Junho. (My birthday is on June 1.)

Eu estarei em casa **em** um mês. (I will be home in one month.)

Eu estudo **durante** os intervalos do meio-dia. (I study during noon breaks.)

A exposição vai durar **até** 31 de Dezembro. (The exhibit will last until December 31st.)

Other Prepositions

de	from (origin, possession)
para	for, in order to
por	for, because of
contra	against
com	with
sem	without
por causa (de)	because of
sobre	about
menos	but, except
conforme, segundo	according (to)
a respeito (de)	concerning, regarding
apesar (de)	in spite of, despite
junto (com)	together (with)

em vez (de)	instead (of)

Esse é o carro **de** Reynaldo. (That is Reynaldo's car.)

A tabela antiga é **da** Itália. (The antique table is from Italy.)

Eu sobrevivi **sem** dinheiro durante um mês. (I survived without money for one month.)

Ele fala sobre sua cidade natal a maior parte do tempo. (He talks about his hometown most of the time.)

Ele se queixou **sobre** a refeição sem graça. (He complained about the bland meal.)

Prepositional Contractions

Some prepositions contract when used before definite articles.

Em -> in, on, at

Contraction with Definite Articles

	Masculine		Feminine		English
	Singular	Plural	Singular	Plural	
Definite articles	o	os	a	as	
Em +	no	nos	na	nas	on/in/at+the

Contraction with Indefinite Articles

	Masculine		Feminine		English
	Singular	Plural	Singular	Plural	
Indefinite articles	um	uns	uma	umas	
Em +	num	nuns	numa	numas	on/in/at+a/some

Examples:

Eu estou **numa** praia. -> I'm in a beach.

Estou **no** restaurant, -> I'm at the restaurant.

Por -> for/through/by

	Masculine		Feminine		English
	Singular	Plural	Singular	Plural	
Definite Articles	o	os	a	as	
Por +	pelo	pelos	pela	pelas	for/through/by+the

Examples:

Enviei seu presente de aniversário **pelo** correio. (I sent your birthday gift by post.)

Eu andei **pelos** campos. (I walked across the fields.)

De -> of/from

Contraction with definite articles:

	Masculine		Feminine		English
	Singular	Plural	Singular	Plural	
Definite Articles	o	os	a	as	
de+	do	dos	da	das	of/from + the

Examples:

(Eu) sou da França. -> I am from France.

(Eu) gosto do carro novo. -> I like the new car.

A -> at, to

The preposition "a" only contracts with definite articles.

	Masculine		Feminine		English
	Singular	Plural	Singular	Plural	
Definite Articles	o	os	a	as	
a+	ao	aos	à	às	at/to + the

Eu raramente ir ao teatro. -> I rarely go to the theater.

Chapter 20: Useful Phrases

Introductions:

Como se chama?	What is you name?
O meu nome é _(state your name)_.	My name is ____.
Chamo-me _(state your name)_. *Inf*	My name is ____.
Este é o meu marido.	This is my husband.
Esta é a minha mulher.	This is my wife.
Esta é a minha filha.	This is my daughter.
Este é o meu filho.	This is my son.
Este é _(name)_.	This is ____.
De onde é?	Where are you from?
Que idade tem?	How old are you?
Tenho _(your age)_ anos.	I'm ___ years old.

Asking for Directions

Como chego ao (à) _(destination)_? -> How do I get to _(destination)_?

Places to see:

aeroporto	the airport
a estação de autocarro	the bus station
estação de comboio	the train station
centro	downtown
hotel	hotel
museu	museum
parquet	park
o consulado	consulate
loja de departamento	department store
bar/bares	bar/bars
restaurante/ restaurantes	restaurant/ restaurants
praia	beach
biblioteca	library
teatro	theater
cathedral	cathedral
igreja	churh
palácio	palace
galeria de arte	art gallery

Useful terms:

Onde é ___ ?	Where is ___ ?
É longe?	Is it far?
Vire à esquerda (veer-eeh ah eh-sskehr-dah)	turn left
Vire à direita (veer-eeh ah dee-ray–tah)	turn right
Esquerda (esh-KER-da)	left
Direita (dee-ray-tah)	right
sempre em frente	straight ahead
em direcção à ___	towards the ___
Depois do(a) ___ (deh-poyss doh/dah)	past the ___
Antes do(a) ___ (ahn-tiss doh/da)	before the ___
Fique atento à ___	watch for the ___
rua (who-ah)	street
Oeste	west
Este	east
Norte	north
Sul	south
descida	downhill
subida	uphill
cruzamento	intersection

The Weather:

Que dia bonito!	What a lovely day!
Que tempo horrível!	What a bad weather!
Vai chover?	Is it going to rain?
Está sol.	It's sunny.
Está quente.	It's hot.
Está encoberto.	It's cloudy.
Está frio.	It's cold.
Está um gelo.	It's freezing.
Está a chover.	It's raining.
Está ventoso.	It's windy.

Eating Out:

Tem uma mesa livre?	Is there an available table?
Gostaria de uma mesa para ___.	I'd like a table for ___.
A ementa, por favor.	The menu, please.
Gostaria de ___.	I'd like ___.
Desejo ___.	I want ___.
Mais pão, por favor.	More bread, please.
Eu sou vegetariano.	I'm a vegetarian.
prato-feito	fixed-price meal
pela ementa	a la carte
breakfast	desjejum, café da manhã
lunch	almoço
janta	dinner
ceia	supper
merenda da tarde	afternoon snack

Não como carne.	I don't eat meat.
O que recomenda?	What do you recommend?
Aproveite a refeição!	Enjoy your meal!
Eu acabar.	I'm finished.
Estava delicioso.	That was delicious.
Está delicioso!	It's delicious!
A conta, por favor.	The bill, please.

Foods to Order:

frango	chicken
bacon	bacon
bife	steak
camarões, gambás	shrimp
peixe	fish
sardinha	sardine
bacalhau	cod
atum	tuna
lula	squid
polvo	octopus
caracóis	snails
anchovas	anchovies
cabra	goat
caril de carne	meat curry
caril de galinha	chicken curry
carne	meat
cordeiro	lamb
hambúrguer	beefburger
porco	pork
presunto	ham
salsicha	sausage
vitela	veal
arroz	rice
batatas	fritas chips
caril	curry
gelado	ice-cream
manteiga	butter
omelete	omelette
ovo	egg
pão	bread
queijo	cheese
salada	salad

sopa	soup
açúcar	sugar
sal	salt
pimenta	pepper

Drinks:

uma garrafa do/de ____	a bottle of ____
um copo do/de ____	a glass of ____
uma cerveja	a beer
um vinho tinto	a red wine
um vinho branco	a white wine
wiski	whiskey
um gin tónico	a gin and tonic
com gelo	with ice
água potável	drinking water
leite	milk
café	coffee
chá ("bebida")	tea drink
sumo de ananás	pineapple juice
sumo de manga	mango juice
sumo de laranja (Port.)	orange juice
suco de laranja (Br.)	orange juice
água	water
água tônica	tonic water
gelo em blocos	ice cubes
gelo esmagado	smashed ice

Getting Around:

Bus or train

Quanto custa o bilhete para (destination).

How much is a ticket to ___?

Um bilhete para (destination), por favor.

One ticket to ___, please.

Para onde vai este autocarro/comboio?

Where does this bus/train go?

Onde apanho um autocarro/comboio para (destination)?

Where is the bus/train to ___?

Esse autocarro/comboio pára em (place)?

Does this bus/train stop in ___?

Quando é que sai o autocarro/comboio para place?

When does the bus/train for ___ leave?

Taxi:

Leve-me para o/a (place), se faz favor.	Please take me to ___.
Por favor use o taxímetro.	Please use the meter.
Por favor abrande.	Please slow down.

| Pare aqui. | Stop here. |

Shopping:

Quanta custa é isto?	How much is this?
Isso é muito caro. (Port.)	That's too expensive.
Isso é caro de mais (BR)	That's too expensive.
Não posso pagar isso.	I can't afford it.
Não quero isso.	I don't want it.
Não estou interessado.	I'm not interested.
Pode dar-me um saco?	Can you give me a bag?
Aceitaria ____?	Would you take?
caro	expensive
barato	cheap
Preciso de ____	I need ____

Things to Buy:

creme dental(BR) .	toothpaste
Pasta de dentes (Port)	toothpaste
uma escova dental(BR)	toothbrush
uma escova de dentes (Port)	toothbrush
higiene íntima feminina	tampoons
sabonete	soap
xampú(BR)	shampoo
champô (Port)	shampoo
remédio contra a dor	pain reliever
analgésico(Port)	pain reliever
medicamento estomacal	stomach medicine
uma lamina para barbear	a razor
um guarda-chuva	un umbrella
protector solar	sunblock lotions
um postal	a postcard
selos de correios	postage stamps
células eléctricas	batteries
papel para escrever	writing paper
uma caneta	a pen

Finding a Place to Stay

Há quartos disponíveis?

Do you have any available room?

Quanto custa para (number of persons) pessoa/pessoas por noite?

How much is a room for ____ person/people per night?

Eu vou ficar por (number) noite(s).

I will stay for ____ nights.

O quarto possui ____	Does the room have ____
casa-de-banho	bathroom
chuveiro	shower
condicionado	airconditioning
telefone	telephone
televisão	a television
lencois	bed sheets
cacifos	lockers
cofre	safe

Posso ver o quarto?	Can I see the room?
Tem um quarto ____ ?	Do you have a ____ room?
mais silencioso	quiter
maior	bigger

mais limpo	cleaner
Ok, eu aceito.	Ok, I'll take it.
Gosto do quarto.	I like the room.
Quero fazer o check-out.	I want to check out.

Money:

Aceita dólares americanos/canadianos/australianos?

Do you accept American/Canadian/Australian Dollars?

Aceita libras britânicas?

Do you accept British pounds?

Aceita Euros?

Do you accept Euros?

Aceita cartões de crédito?

Do you take credit cards?

Qual é a taxa de câmbio?

What is the exchange rate?

Onde é o multibanco?

Where is the ATM?

Emergency:

Portuguese	English
Onde é o hospital?	Where is the hospital?
Estou perdido.	I'm lost.
Necessito de um medico.	I need a doctor.
Preciso de um medico. (inf.)	I need a doctor.
Houve um acidente.	There has been an accident.
Preciso de ajuda.	I need help.
Ajuda!	Help!
Perdi o meu dinheiro.	I have lost my money.
Perdi o meu passaporte.	I lost my passport.
Perdi a minha carteira.	I have lost my handbag.
Perdi o meu porta-moedas.	I have lost my wallet.
Chame uma ambulância!	Call an ambulance!
Chame a polícia!	Call the police!

Chapter 21: Vocabulary

Os membros da família (The Family Members)

pais (pie-ish)	parents
pai (pie)	father, dad
mãe (mah-ing)	mother, mom
marido (mah-ree-doo)	husband
mulher (moo-lyehr)	wife
Irmãos (eer-maoongsh)	siblings
filha (fee-lyeeah)	daughter
filho (fee-lyeeoh)	son
irmã (eer-mah)	sister
irmão (eer-maung)	brother
avós (ah-vÓsh)	grandparents
avó (ah-vÓH)	grandmother
avô (ah-voh)	grandfather
netos (neh-toosh)	grandchildren
neta (neh-tah)	granddaughter
neto (neh-too)	grandson
tia (tee-ah)	aunt
tio (tee-oo)	uncle
primo (pree-moo)	male cousin
prima (pree-mah)	female cousin
sobrinha (soo-bree-nyah)	niece
sobrinho (soo-bree-nyoh)	nephew
sogra (soh-grah)	mother-in-law
sogro (soh-groo)	father-in-law
nora (noh-rah)	daughter-in-law

genro (jaing-rooh)	son-in-law
cunhada (coo-nyah-dah)	sister-in-law
cunhado (coo-nyah-doo)	brother-in-law
namorado (Na-moo-rah-doo)	boyfriend
namorada (Na-moo-rah-dah)	girlfriend
companheiro (com-pah-nyaee-roo)	male partner
companheira (com-pah-nyaee-rah)	female partner
noiva (noee-vah)	fiancée (female)
noivo (noee-voo)	fiancé (male)

As Profissões (The Professions)

o contabilista	accountant
o ator	actor
o arquiteto	architect
o artista	artist
o talhante	butcher
o chefe de cozinha	chef
o dentista	dentist
o detetive	detective
o médico	doctor
o condutor	driver
o eletricista	electrician
o engenheiro	engineer
o agricultor	farmer
o bombeiro	fireman
o pescador	fisherman
o cabeleireiro	hairdresser
o caçador	hunter
o juiz	judge
o advogado	lawyer
o mecânico	mechanic
o modelo	model
o músico	musician
o enfermeiro	nurse
o pintor	painter
o farmacêutico	pharmacist
o fotógrafo	photographer
o piloto	pilot
o canalizador	plumber
o polícia	policeman

o político	politician
o marinheiro	sailor
o cientista	scientist
o cantor	singer
o soldado	soldier
o treinador	trainer
o veterinário	vet (veterinarian)
o empregado	waiter

Partes do corpo (Parts of the Body)

o braço	arm
as costas	back
o corpo	body
o rabo	bottom
a bochecha	cheek
o peito	chest
a orelha	ear
o cotovelo	elbow
o olho	eye
a sobrancelha	eyebrow
a face	face
o dedo	finger
a unha	finger nail
o pé	foot
o cabelo	hair
a mão	hand
a cabeça	head
o coração	heart
a anca	hip
o maxilar	jaw
o joelho	knee
a perna	leg
o lábio	lip
o pulmão	lung
a boca	mouth
o pescoço	neck
o nariz	nose
o ombro	shoulder
a pele	skin
o estômago	stomach
a coxa	thigh

a garganta	throat
o polegar	thumb
o dedo	toe
a língua	tongue
o dente	tooth

Os Animais (The Animals)

a formiga	ant
o urso	bear
a abelha	bee
o pássaro	bird
a borboleta	butterfly
o camelo	camel
o gato	cat
a galinha	chicken
a vaca	cow
o caranguejo	crab
o veado	deer
o cão	dog
o pato	duck
o peixe	fish
a rã	frog
a cabra	goat
o ganso	goose
o cavalo	horse
o lagarto	lizard
o macaco	monkey
o rato	mouse
o polvo	octopus
o porco	pig
o coelho	rabbit
a ovelha	sheep
a cobra	snake
a aranha	spider
o cisne	swan
o peru	turkey
a baleia	whale

O Roupeiro (The Wardrobe)

o cinto	belt
a bota	boot
o soutien	bra
a pulseira	bracelet
o boné	cap
o casaco	coat
o vestido	dress
os brincos	earring
os óculos	glasses
a luva	glove
a mala	handbag
o lenço	handkerchief
o cabide	hanger
o chapéu	hat
o casaco	jacket
as calças de ganga	jeans
o colar	necklace
as calças	pants
o anel	ring
o lenço	scarf
a camisa	shirt
o sapato	shoe
os calções	shorts
a saia	skirt
os ténis	sneaker
a peúga	sock
a meia	stocking
o fato de banho	swimsuit
a gravata	tie
a roupa interior	underwear

o colete	vest
a carteira	wallet
o relógio	watch

As Frutas e Legumes (The Fruits and Vegetables)

a maçã	apple
a banana	banana
o feijão	bean
os brócolos	broccoli
a couve	cabbage
o pimento	capsicum
a cenoura	carrot
a couve-flor	cauliflower
a cereja	cherry
o coco	coconut
o pepino	cucumber
a beringela	eggplant
a uva	grape
o limão	lemon
a alface	lettuce
o melão	melon
o fruto seco	nut
a cebola	onion
a laranja	orange
a ervilha	pea
o pêssego	peach
a pêra	pear
a ameixa	plum
a batata	potato
a ameixa seca	prune
a abóbora	pumpkin
os espinafres	spinach
a sultana	sultana
o tomate	tomato
a melancia	watermelon

Os Tempo (The Weather)

a nuvem	cloud
enublado	cloudy
frio	cold
o ciclone	cyclone
bom	fine
a cheia	flood
o nevoeiro	fog
a geada	frost
o granizo	hail
quente	hot
o relâmpago	lightning
a chuva	rain
o arco-íris	rainbow
chuvoso	rainy
a neve	snow
a tempestade	storm
temporal	stormy
a temperatura	temperature
o trovão	thunder
o tornado	tornado
o vento	wind

Conclusion

I hope this book was able to help you to learn the Portuguese language in the fastest and easiest way.

It's time for you to take up advanced courses in Portuguese, practice what you have learned by conversing with native Portuguese speakers, and perhaps going on a trip to Portuguese-speaking countries.

I wish you the best of luck!

To your success,

Henry Ray